T0329265

CAMBRIDGE CLASSICAL STUDIES V

General Editors

F. M. CORNFORD D. S. ROBERTSON, F. E. ADCOCK

DIONYSIUS OF HALICARNASSUS

THE LITERARY TREATISES OF
DIONYSIUS
OF HALICARNASSUS

A Study in the
Development of Critical Method

BY

S. F. BONNER, M.A.
Lecturer in Latin in the University of Liverpool,
formerly Scholar of Pembroke College, Cambridge

CAMBRIDGE
AT THE UNIVERSITY PRESS
1939

CAMBRIDGE UNIVERSITY PRESS
Cambridge, New York, Melbourne, Madrid, Cape Town,
Singapore, São Paulo, Delhi, Mexico City

Cambridge University Press
The Edinburgh Building, Cambridge CB2 8RU, UK

Published in the United States of America by Cambridge University Press, New York

www.cambridge.org
Information on this title: www.cambridge.org/9781107685444

First published 1939
First paperback edition 2013

A catalogue record for this publication is available from the British Library

ISBN 978-1-107-68544-4 Paperback

CONTENTS

PREFACE

THE nucleus of the present work, together with other material on Greek stylistic theory, formed an essay for which the Cromer Greek Prize was awarded by the British Academy in 1936. Since then I have considerably developed and extended the study, with a view to setting forth in more detail my main contention —namely that there is noticeable throughout the literary treatises of Dionysius a gradual but distinct improvement in thoroughness of critical exposition. A separate study of these essays seemed to me worth making for two reasons: first, Dionysius' critical methods have rarely been subjected to a close examination, and, secondly, there is no full treatment in English of one who, despite his shortcomings, must rank among the best literary critics of antiquity.

In sending forth this *opusculum* upon *opuscula*, I would like to record my appreciation of the valuable work of Rhys Roberts on the Greek critics, and on Dionysius in particular; to his stimulating Introductions I owed my first interest in the subject. My sincere thanks are due to those who have allowed me to benefit by their criticism and advice, namely, Professor J. F. Mountford, of the University of Liverpool, and two of the Editors of this Series, Professors D. S. Robertson and F. E. Adcock. I am further indebted to Professor Mountford, and also to my wife, for considerable assistance in the reading of proofs; and I would also pay a tribute in this respect to the care and accuracy of the Readers of the University Press.

LIVERPOOL   S. F. B.

February, 1939

CHAPTER I

The critic; his environment and equipment

DIONYSIUS of Halicarnassus and Quintus Horatius Flaccus were very close contemporaries,[1] were both keenly interested in literature and literary criticism, were both resident in Rome during the first half of the Augustan Age, and may even have known each other;[2] yet to the modern student of their age they present a remarkable contrast. Horace, by reason of the wealth of personal anecdote and the revealing touches of autobiography which abound in his works, emerges as a real and knowable figure, whose likes and dislikes, foibles, inconsistencies, and delightful philosophy of life are so clearly portrayed as to create a sense of intimacy at once. Dionysius, on the other hand, is known to us only as the scholar, not at all as the man; his reticence concerning his own life and activities is such that we are left the impression of little more than a shadow, moving obscurely in the background of the Augustan Age.

In the Preface to his *Early History of Rome*,[3] a work which he almost certainly regarded as his *magnum opus*,[4] Dionysius tells us that he sailed from his native Halicarnassus to Rome in the middle of the 187th Olympiad (i.e. in 30 B.C.), at the close of the Civil Wars. There he devoted himself to the study of Roman history, and, after twenty-two years of research, produced the voluminous work,

---

[1] Horace was born in 65 B.C., and Dionysius probably not much later than 60. The evidence for the date of Dionysius' birth is of a very general nature, and is examined by H. Dodwell, *De Aetate Dionysii Halicarnassei*, in the editions of Hudson (1704) and Reiske (1774-7); see also Max. Egger, *Denys d'Halicarnasse* (Paris, 1902), p. 3.

[2] G. C. Fiske, *Lucilius and Horace* (Madison, 1920), p. 77, states this as a fact; it is, of course, purely conjectural.

[3] *Ant. Rom.* I, 7.

[4] Cf. W. Rhys Roberts, *Dionysius of Halicarnassus: the Three Literary Letters* (Cambridge, 1901), p. 4. So Strabo, Dionysius' contemporary, refers to him, not as a critic, but as a historian (XIV, p. 656 καθ' ἡμᾶς Διονύσιος ὁ συγγραφεύς).

of which little more than one half has survived. The composition of his *History* necessitated a knowledge of the Latin language, and this, he informs us, he acquired during his stay; but, more than this, it brought him into close contact with many contemporary scholars and men of letters.[1] That Dionysius was thoroughly at home in the metropolis is clear from the fact that he desired his *History*, when it appeared, to be regarded as a thank-offering for the kindly treatment he had received.[2]

In Rome Dionysius also practised as a teacher of rhetoric; and, though he does not appear to have been conspicuous as a *declamator*, he clearly acted as tutor to Roman youths, and possibly kept an open school.[3] In his treatise on literary composition, which he addresses as a birthday-gift to his young pupil Metilius (or Melitius)[4] Rufus, Dionysius promises to expound certain points more fully ἐν ταῖς καθ᾽ ἡμέραν γυμνασίαις,[5] and it was his activity as a teacher of rhetoric which led him to study the works of the Attic orators, on whose characteristics he makes so many illuminating remarks.

It is a very probable assumption that the literary treatises which claim our present attention were written at intervals during the period in which Dionysius was engaged in writing the *History*.[6] Indeed, they bear many signs of rapid composition,[7] though it is

---

[1] *Ant. Rom., loc. cit.* καὶ τὰ μὲν παρὰ τῶν λογιωτάτων ἀνδρῶν, οἷς εἰς ὁμιλίαν ἦλθον, διδαχῇ παραλαβών.

[2] *Ib.* I, 6 χαριστηρίους ἀμοιβάς, ἃς ἐμοὶ δύναμις ἦν, ἀποδοῦναι τῇ πόλει, παιδείας τε μεμνημένῳ καὶ τῶν ἄλλων ἀγαθῶν ὅσων ἀπέλαυσα διατρίψας ἐν αὐτῇ.

[3] Cf. F. Blass, *Die griechische Beredsamkeit in dem Zeitraum von Alexander bis auf Augustus* (Berlin, 1865), p. 172; Christ-Schmid-Stählin, *Geschichte der griechischen Litteratur*, II, I, § 566; Egger, *op. cit.* p. 7, doubts whether Dionysius had a school.

[4] The MS. readings at *De Comp. Verb.* c. I are divided, but Metilius is the more probable, being the name of a Republican *gens*; a M. Metilius Rufus, governor of Achaea, appears in I.G. III, 874.

[5] *De Comp. Verb.* c. 20 (= II, 94, Usener-Radermacher).

[6] Roberts, *op. cit.* p. 5; Egger, *op. cit.* pp. 20–2.

[7] Cf. *De Lys.* c. 10 (= I, 17) τοῦ χρόνου στοχαζόμενος; *De Isocrate* c. 20 (= I, 92) ἀνάγκη δὲ ἴσως στοχάζεσθαι τοῦ χρόνου; *De Isaeo*, c. 15 (= I, 114); *De Dem.* c. 14 (= I, 159); c. 32 (= I, 201).

only fair to their author to admit that they rarely betray carelessness or inconsistency. It is a recurring characteristic of Dionysius to promise a separate treatise on a point which he feels himself unable to elucidate fully at the time;[1] and the fact that some of these promised essays do not appear to have been composed agrees with the supposition that the extant *Scripta Rhetorica* were the work of one whose leisure hours were all too few.

Considerable light might be thrown on the life of Dionysius if only more could be discovered about those personal friends to whom he dedicated his essays as they appeared;[2] but enough can be gathered from his references to them to warrant the belief that Dionysius was, if not the central figure, at least a very active member of one of the literary coteries which were so marked a feature of the period in which he wrote. His essays suggest that constant interchange of opinion took place between himself and interested friends,[3] while not infrequently one may discern the signs of a literary polemic. Among the most intimate of these students of literature was Ammaeus, the φίλτατος, κράτιστος, and βέλτιστος 'Αμμαῖος to whom Dionysius addresses one of his most ambitious works, the treatise on the ancient orators. Ammaeus seems to have been particularly familiar with Demosthenes, the idol of Dionysius; for not only is he mentioned in one passage as being occupied with this author,[4] but it is he who brings to Dionysius' notice the view of a certain contemporary Peripatetic philosopher who had asserted that the speeches of Demosthenes were based upon a careful observance of the rules laid down in the *Rhetoric* of Aristotle—a view which Dionysius, in his extant reply to Ammaeus, soundly and convincingly rejects.[5] It was also at Ammaeus' request for a fuller explanation of the views

---

[1] *De Lys.* c. 12 (= I, 22); c. 14 (= I, 25); *De Isaeo*, c. 2 (= I, 94); *De Dem.* c. 32 (= I, 201); *Ep. ad Amm.* I, 3 (= I, 259); *De Comp. Verb.* c. I (= II, 5).

[2] See especially W. Rhys Roberts, "The Literary Circle of Dionysius of Halicarnassus", *C.R.* xiv (1900), pp. 439–42.

[3] Cf. below, p. 5.

[4] *De Dem.* c. 13 (= I, 156) οἷς (*sc.* τοῖς τοῦ Δημοσθένους ἰδιωτικοῖς λόγοις) γε δὴ κατὰ τὸ παρὸν ἐντετυχηκὼς γνώσῃ ὁποῖα λέγω.

[5] *Ep. ad Amm.* I *init.* (= I, 257), πρώτως ἀκούσαντι παρὰ σοῦ, ὅτι τῶν φιλοσόφων τις κ.τ.λ.

which Dionysius had expressed on the style of Thucydides, that a second "literary letter" was composed.[1] But quite apart from the letters which bear the name of Ammaeus, the modern reader of Dionysius probably owes more than he realises to the pertinent questions of this contemporary scholar.[2]

The long-standing quarrel between philosophers and rhetoricians, in which a new note was struck by the first letter to Ammaeus, is again echoed in the letter addressed by Dionysius to Pompeius Geminus. Pompeius (who was possibly influenced by Poseidonius) possessed so keen an admiration for Plato that he felt himself bound to oppose the view expressed by Dionysius in his essay on Demosthenes that Plato's style was not free from serious faults; and he is thereby responsible for the third literary letter, in which Dionysius replies to his objections and maintains his own position.[3] To Pompeius' request for the critic's opinion of the historians, particularly Herodotus and Xenophon, we owe an excerpt of considerable length concerning them from the second book of the work on imitation;[4] this excerpt Dionysius appended to his reply concerning Plato, and apart from a few scattered fragments,[5] it is the only part of the essay on imitation which survives in its original form.[6]

To pass from Ammaeus and Pompeius Geminus to Quintus Aelius Tubero, at whose request Dionysius composed a special essay on Thucydides, is to pass from two Greeks of unknown origin and connections[7] to a Roman who attained to some distinction under

[1] *Ep. ad Amm.* II init. (= I, 421) σοῦ δὲ ὑπολαμβάνοντος ἧττον ἠκριβῶσθαι τὰς γραφάς κ.τ.λ.

[2] Cf. *De Dem.* c. 13 (= I, 157) ἀξιοῖς γὰρ δὴ καὶ τοῦτο μαθεῖν (*sc.* πῇ κρείττων ἐστὶ Λυσίου Δημοσθένης), and especially *Ep. ad Amm.* I, c. 2 (= I, 258) where Ammaeus is clearly the instigator.

[3] *Ep. ad Pomp.* cc. 1–2 (= II, 221 ff.).   [4] *Ib.* cc. 3–6 (= II, 232 ff.).

[5] Collected by C. T. Roessler, *D.H. Scriptorum Rhetoricorum Fragmenta* (Leipzig, 1873), pp. 26 ff., followed by Usener, *D.H. Librorum De Imitatione Reliquiae Epistulaeque Criticae Duae* (Bonn, 1889) (cf. II, 197 ff.).

[6] A later epitome of Book II exists; discovered by H. Stephanus in 1554, and long printed as the *Veterum Censura*, it has been edited by Usener, *op. cit.*

[7] Pompeius Geminus is conjectured to have been a freedman of the great Pompey by Krüger, *Dion. Hal., Historiographica* (Halle, 1823), p. 3 (following Reiske). For his possible authorship of the Περὶ Ὕψους, see G. C. Richards, *C.Q.* XXXII (1938), pp. 133–4.

the Augustan régime. Tubero may well have been the younger of the two Tuberones who attacked the Ligarius defended by Cicero in 46 B.C.,[1] and is possibly to be identified with the consul of 11 B.C. As a jurist and historian, connected with one of the leading Roman families, Tubero was clearly a man of standing, with whom Dionysius was probably on somewhat less familiar terms; and this is to some little extent borne out by the essay on Thucydides, in which Tubero is addressed as one who merits consideration and respect.[2]

With Tubero may be classed the father of that Metilius Rufus who has been mentioned already as the recipient of the De Compositione Verborum; he is to Dionysius τιμιώτατος φίλων,[3] words which perhaps hardly lend themselves to the supposition that he was a patron to whose favour Dionysius was indebted.

Enough, then, can be gathered from the circumstances in which the essays were written to make it clear that they were primarily intended for those ψυχαὶ εὐπαίδευτοι καὶ μέτριαι[4] who formed a literary circle of educated Greeks and Romans, though there are not lacking references which strongly suggest that they were ultimately destined for a wider public.[5] Within the circle itself there was considerable interchange of literary documents; for it is noteworthy that the essays on the ancient orators, originally addressed to Ammaeus, found their way into the hands of a certain Zeno, who transmitted them to Pompeius Geminus,[6] while the essay on Thucydides, composed for Tubero, was also read by Ammaeus.

With the exception of the Demetrius to whom the essay on imitation was addressed,[7] and of whom nothing whatever is known,[8]

---

[1] Cf. Pro Ligario, passim.

[2] Cf. Roberts, op. cit. p. 441; Egger, op. cit. pp. 8 and 10.

[3] De Comp. Verb. c. 1 (= II, 4).   [4] De Lys. c. 20 (= I, 32).

[5] De Dem. c. 32 (= I, 201); De Thuc. c. 2 (= I, 326 and 328); ib. c. 25 (= I, 364) and c. 35 (= I, 383).

[6] Ep. ad Pomp. c. 1 (= II, 221) τὰς συντάξεις τὰς ἐμὰς ἐπιχορηγοῦντός σοι Ζήνωνος τοῦ κοινοῦ φίλου διαπορευόμενος κ.τ.λ.

[7] Ib. c. 3 (= II, 232).

[8] Roberts, op. cit. pp. 440-1, conjectures that he may have been the author of the Περὶ Ἑρμηνείας wrongly ascribed to Demetrius of Phalerum; but there is no evidence, and Roberts himself indulges in quite another fancy in his Greek Rhetoric and Literary Criticism (London and N.Y. 1928), p. 70.

the only remaining name which occurs in the *Scripta Rhetorica* is that of Caecilius, who is a so much more tangible figure than those mentioned hitherto that he is deserving of especial consideration.[1] According to Suidas (whose account, however, is not free from serious blunders[2]), Caecilius of Calacte, a Sicilian by birth, and by faith a Jew, practised as a rhetorician in Rome under Augustus, and composed numerous works of a literary and historical character. His literary works, of which Suidas gives a list, may be divided into those of a purely technical character, such as a lexicon of rhetorical terms, a glossary of Attic phrases, an art of rhetoric, and a treatise on figures, and those which are classed more properly under the heading of "literary criticism", such as the work on the characteristics of the ten orators, separate essays on Antiphon[3] and Lysias, comparisons between Demosthenes and Aeschines, and between Demosthenes and Cicero. To the latter class also belonged the treatise *On the Sublime*, which inspired the eloquent rejoinder of "Longinus", while two essays *Against the Phrygians* and *On the difference between the Attic and the Asiatic style* bordered very closely upon the same type of composition.

A much-vexed question is that concerning the relations which existed between Caecilius and Dionysius; according to some[4] they were friendly collaborators; according to others[5] they were rival professors whose opinions constantly differed. There are admittedly two fragments of Caecilius which do reveal differences of opinion; of these the first[6] proves a disagreement regarding the order of the

---

[1] On Caecilius see Brzoska's valuable article in Pauly-Wissowa's *Real-Encyclopädie*; fragments are collected in E. Ofenloch, *Caecilii Calactini Fragmenta* (Teubner, Leipzig, 1907); cf. also W. Rhys Roberts, in *A.J.P.* XVII (1897), pp. 302–12; further literature in Brzoska, Ofenloch, and Lehnert's reports in Bursian.

[2] Blass, *op. cit.* p. 174.

[3] Cf. below, p. 9, n. 4.

[4] Blass, *op. cit.* p. 175; Roberts, *op. cit.* p. 303; J. Tolkiehn, *W.kl.Ph.* 1908, pp. 84–6; Christ-Schmid-Stählin, *op. cit.* p. 463, n. 8.

[5] Ofenloch, *op. cit. prooemium* XIII, XXVII, XXX; von Wilamowitz-Möllendorff in *Abhandlungen der Gesellschaft der Wissenschaft zu Göttingen, phil.-hist. Klasse*, N.F. IV, 3, p. 70; K. Münscher in *Philologus*, LVIII (1899), p. 109.

[6] Schol. *ad Dem. Ol.* II *init.* (p. 71, 1 Dind.) (= frag. 136, Ofenloch).

Olynthiacs of Demosthenes, the second[1] shows a small divergency
concerning the number of the genuine speeches of Isocrates. But to
make these differences a starting-point for arguing that when later
writers record disagreement with Dionysius they are representing
the views of Caecilius[2], is a dangerous and unwarrantable procedure.
To balance such divergencies of opinion, several instances of definite
agreement can be adduced. In the first place, Dionysius expressly
records his agreement with his "dear Caecilius"[3] about the influence
of Thucydides on Demosthenes; and to assume that φίλτατος
Καικίλιος is ironical or merely a courtesy-phrase[4] is perverse in view
of the fact that nowhere in the *Scripta Rhetorica* does Dionysius use
φίλος or φίλτατος to connote anything but sincere friendship.[5]
Secondly, we know from pseudo-Plutarch (*De Vit. X Or.* p. 836 a)[6]
that Dionysius and Caecilius agreed in their estimate of the
number of speeches genuinely attributable to Lysias—hardly a
fortuitous concurrence; and the expression there used, οἱ περὶ
Διονύσιον καὶ Καικίλιον, strongly suggests that the two were regarded
as authorities, the results of whose investigations were in harmony.
Thirdly, we know from Photius[7] (p. 489 b) that Caecilius acknowledged Lysias to be lacking in power of arrangement (οἰκονομία),
though abundantly supplied with ideas (εὕρεσις); this statement is in
exact agreement with the remarks of Dionysius, who in *De Lysia*,
c. 15 *sub fin.*, praises the εὕρεσις of Lysias, but advises his pupils to
turn to other models for better οἰκονομία. It is noteworthy in this
connection that mention of this criticism of Lysias is made by a
Neoplatonic scholiast on the *Phaedrus*,[8] who attributes it to οἱ
κριτικοί, which would therefore seem to mean particularly Dionysius
and Caecilius. Finally, the two critics stood closely together in

[1] Pseudo-Plutarch, *De Vit. X Or.* p. 838 d (= frag. 117, Ofenloch).
[2] E.g. fragments 110, 142, 146; see Ofenloch, xxvii.
[3] *Ep. ad Pomp.* c. 3 (= II, 240) ἐμοὶ μέντοι καὶ τῷ φιλτάτῳ Καικιλίῳ
δοκεῖ κ.τ.λ.
[4] Münscher, *loc. cit.*, "wohl nur ein Höflichkeitsphrase".
[5] I, 236; II, 226 (φίλτατος); I, 259, 438 (φίλος).
[6] Ofenloch, frag. 108.
[7] Ofenloch, frag. 110.
[8] Hermeias Alexandrinus on *Phaedrus*, p. 236 A (= Ofenloch, frag.
110 a).

their estimate of the style of Plato.[1] Dionysius, in his essay on the style of Demosthenes, admitted that Plato had the power to write remarkably pure, direct, lucid, and pleasant Greek,[2] but considered him deserving of the strongest censure for his frequent employment of metaphors and poetical figures, which rendered him obscure.[3] Caecilius, too, spoke of the accuracy, purity, simplicity, and rhythm of the prose of Plato,[4] but severely criticised him for his strong and harsh metaphors and inflated allegory, and was even led so far as to account Lysias altogether superior to Plato.[5] Thus we see that there is considerable evidence for believing the two scholars to have been in agreement on various points of criticism.

However, it would obviously be dangerous, even if instances of agreement or disagreement on such matters of scholarly opinion could be multiplied, to infer therefrom agreement or disagreement in aims and outlook. More revealing than small agreements or divergencies is the fact that both Dionysius and Caecilius were avowed enemies of the Asiatic style; if the titles of Caecilius' works *Against the Phrygians* and *On the difference between the Attic and the Asiatic style* be considered alongside the Preface of Dionysius to his treatise on the orators, where he expresses the deepest disgust with Asianism, "that Mysian or Phrygian or Carian bane",[6] it will be realised that the two critics were inspired by a common purpose in dealing with one of the major problems of their day. From the

---

[1] Cf. F. Nassal, *Aesthetisch-Rhetorische Beziehungen zwischen Dionysius von Halicarnass und Cicero* (Tübingen, 1910), pp. 161–2. (Nassal's hypothesis, however, that C. is the common source of Dionysius and Cicero, breaks down in face of Cicero's enthusiasm for Plato; there are also difficulties of date.) Cf. also F. Walsdorff, *Die antiken Urteile über Platons Stil* (Bonn, 1927), p. 30.

[2] c. 5 (= I, 136) ὅταν μὲν οὖν τὴν ἰσχνὴν καὶ ἀφελῆ καὶ ἀποίητον ἐπιτηδεύῃ φράσιν, ἐκτόπως ἡδεῖά ἐστι καὶ φιλάνθρωπος κ.τ.λ.

[3] *Ib.* (= I, 137) ὅταν δὲ εἰς τὴν περιττολογίαν καὶ τὸ καλλιεπεῖν... ἄμετρον ὁρμὴν λάβῃ, πολλῷ χείρων ἑαυτῆς γίνεται... μάλιστα δὲ χειμάζεται περὶ τὴν τροπικὴν φράσιν.

[4] Ofenloch, frag. 126a οὐδὲν τοῦ χαρακτῆρος τοῦ Πλατωνικοῦ σῴζει (sc. ὁ Αἰσχίνης), οὔτε τὸ ἀκριβὲς καὶ καθαρὸν καὶ ἀπέριττον ⟨οὔτε τὸ μεγαλοπρεπὲς καὶ *⟩ καὶ εὔρυθμον.

[5] [Longinus] Π. Ὕψ. c. 32 (= frag. 150, Ofenloch).

[6] I, 4 Μυσὴ ἢ Φρυγία τις ἢ Καρικόν τι κακόν; cf. Cic. *Orator*, § 25.

statement of the author of the Περὶ Ὕψους (c. 32) that Caecilius was inordinately fond of Lysias, and from the fact that Caecilius devoted a special treatise to this author, the assumption has been made that he was an Atticist of the extremist set. Yet this is an unsafe argument, for, in the first place, it should be remembered that the Περὶ Ὕψους is a polemical treatise directed against Caecilius himself[1]— and its value as evidence is not a little impaired by the fragment already quoted which proves Caecilius to have admitted a deficiency in Lysias;[2] while, secondly, the publication by Caecilius of a separate treatise or treatises on, or in defence of,[3] Lysias should not be over-stressed, in view of the fact that Caecilius wrote at least two special treatises concerning Demosthenes, and probably also a special work on Antiphon,[4] and was clearly interested in all the orators. To describe Caecilius therefore as "ein allzu fanatischer Attiker"[5] is to transcend the limits of reasonable deduction; both he and Dionysius regarded all the orators as possessing some qualities worthy of imitation for the cultivation of a good prose style.

Finally, one may observe a further point of contact between Dionysius and Caecilius in their common use of the comparative method in literary criticism. Dionysius in his essay on the style of Demosthenes compares Thucydides, Lysias, Isocrates, and Plato in turn with Demosthenes, and finds something unsatisfactory in all but the master-orator; so Caecilius compared Demosthenes with Aeschines, and, in a more daring effort which drew caustic comments from Plutarch,[6] Demosthenes with Cicero. The extensive use of comparative criticism was one of the most promising departures

[1] Cf. Roberts, *op. cit.* p. 306.
[2] Cf. Brzoska, *op. cit.* col. 1184 "strenger Lysianer nach dem Muster der von Cicero oft verspotteten Attiker par excellence war er deshalb nicht".
[3] If the use of the plural and the preposition are to be stressed in Π. Ὕψ. c. 32.
[4] Cf. pseudo-Plutarch, *De Vit. X Or.* p. 832 e (= Ofenloch, frag. 99). This fragment points to a separate work, and should not be classed as referring to the treatise Περὶ τοῦ χαρακτῆρος τῶν δέκα ῥητόρων. So Blass, *Attische Beredsamkeit* I², 118; Roberts, *op. cit.* p. 305.
[5] Wilamowitz-Möllendorff, *Die griechische Literatur des Altertums*, [= Kultur der Gegenwart, 1, 8] (Berlin and Leipzig, 1905), p. 148.
[6] *Vit. Dem.* c. 3; cf. Roberts, *op. cit.* p. 310.

made by these Augustan critics and affords a further indication of their common purpose and method.[1]

With Caecilius the literary circle of Dionysius is—so far as it can be reconstructed—complete; and although it is highly probable that he met many other scholars and men of letters, particularly in the new libraries which were so striking a feature of Augustan Rome,[2] there is a complete dearth of further evidence. Nor indeed is it known whether Dionysius stayed in Rome after the publication of his *History* in 8 B.C., nor when he died. One thing, however, is clear: that is, that during his prolonged stay, he found himself fully in sympathy with Augustus and his ministers in their desire to uplift the standards of literature and eloquence. It is to them, in no uncertain terms, that he gives the credit for the revival which had already taken place when he wrote; and, viewing the increasing output of good contemporary literature, both Greek and Roman, he prophesies success for their efforts in oratory, history, and philosophy alike.[3] However, this sympathy with the views of the leaders of the state will appear in a clearer light from a consideration of the aims of Dionysius as a rhetorician and literary critic; these aims are easily discoverable in his essays, and claim all the closer attention in that they may be expected to have affected the nature, if not the actual quality, of his critical work.

Much of Dionysius' work, particularly that which was concerned with the establishment of lists of genuine and spurious speeches,[4]

[1] Incidental comparisons are, of course, common long before the Augustan Age. An early example is seen in the fragment of Demetrius Magnes quoted in c. 1 of the *De Dinarcho*.

[2] Cf. Egger, *op. cit.* p. 5.

[3] *Proem*, c. 3 (= 1, 5) αἰτία δ' οἶμαι καὶ ἀρχὴ τῆς τοσαύτης μεταβολῆς ἐγένετο ἡ πάντων κρατοῦσα Ῥώμη πρὸς ἑαυτὴν ἀναγκάζουσα τὰς ὅλας πόλεις ἀποβλέπειν καὶ ταύτης δὲ αὐτῆς οἱ δυναστεύοντες κατ' ἀρετὴν καὶ ἀπὸ τοῦ κρατίστου τὰ κοινὰ διοικοῦντες, εὐπαίδευτοι πάνυ καὶ γενναῖοι τὰς κρίσεις γενόμενοι, ὑφ' ὧν κοσμούμενον τό τε φρόνιμον τῆς πόλεως μέρος ἔτι μᾶλλον ἐπιδέδωκεν καὶ τὸ ἀνόητον ἠνάγκασται νοῦν ἔχειν. τοιγάρτοι πολλαὶ μὲν ἱστορίαι σπουδῆς ἄξιαι γράφονται τοῖς νῦν, πολλοὶ δὲ λόγοι πολιτικοὶ χαρίεντες ἐκφέρονται φιλόσοφοί τε συντάξεις οὐ μὰ Δία εὐκαταφρόνητοι ἄλλαι τε πολλαὶ καὶ καλαὶ πραγματεῖαι καὶ Ῥωμαίοις καὶ Ἕλλησιν εὖ μάλα διεσπουδασμέναι προεληλύθασί τε καὶ προελεύσονται κατὰ τὸ εἰκός.

[4] See especially the *Tabulae Criticae Orationum Atticarum* (including the *De Dinarcho*) printed in 1, 283 ff. of Usener-Radermacher's text.

must have proceeded originally from the scholar's desire to attain to accuracy and truth in his researches. Not that such work did not have a considerable practical value; for it was obviously of service to all students of oratory to know when they were dealing with a genuine speech of one of the great orators, and when they were merely being deceived by one of those servile imitations which circulated all too freely in the Hellenistic world, and brought no little profit to those who compiled them.[1] But such *Echtheitskritik* could flourish among scholars quite out of touch with the citizen community, as it did at Alexandria and Pergamum. In his literary essays of a wider scope Dionysius had an aim which was intensely practical, and which was closely bound up with the exercise of his profession as an active rhetorician in the metropolis. He was not a solitary worker; he was actively connected with the movement for improvement of character, encouraged by the régime under which he lived. So in his essay on Isocrates he claims that such virtues as patriotism, justice, piety, and self-restraint are inculcated by a study of that author, and his enthusiastic treatment of the moral value of Isocrates, at somewhat disproportionate length, strongly suggests that he was consciously producing propaganda for the Augustan programme of moral reform. It was not enough, then, for Dionysius that the study of rhetoric should mean the mere mastering of a technique, however detailed, within the walls of the school; he desired that it should help to foster πολιτικὴ φιλοσοφία in the minds of his students, that is, a broad and intelligent conception of their duties as citizens.[2] It was in defence of this ideal that he composed a treatise, highly polemical in character, which has not survived, entitled Ὑπὲρ τῆς πολιτικῆς φιλοσοφίας πρὸς τοὺς κατατρέχοντας αὐτῆς ἀδίκως,[3] in which he probably attacked members of the Epicurean school,[4] notorious as it was for its lack of interest in

---

[1] On such profitable imitations see *De Thuc.* c. 52 (= 1, 411), and for bad imitations in general *De Dinarcho*, c. 8 (= 1, 307–8).

[2] See especially the passage of the *De Isocrate* (c. 4) translated below (p. 12), and cf. H. M. Hubbell, *The Influence of Isocrates on Cicero, Dionysius and Aristides* (Yale University Press, 1914), pp. 41–53.

[3] *De Thuc.* c. 2 (= 1, 327).

[4] Philodemus and his sect are suggested by Usener (*Praef.* p. xxxv), who is followed by Radermacher (*PW.* v, col. 962), and Roberts (edition of *De Comp. Verb.* p. 250).

political life. If so, this would be the work which Diogenes Laertius (x, 4) had in mind when he numbered Dionysius among the enemies of Epicurus.[1]

For this conception of rhetoric as subordinate to citizenship Dionysius may possibly have Stoic teachers to thank, though the point of view is ultimately that of Isocrates.[2] But whatever the precise influences which helped to shape Dionysius' views in this matter, it is at least to his credit that he is no mere theoretician, no devotee of a narrow cult such as that of the followers of Apollodorus and Theodorus, but a believer in the necessity for cultivation of the character and enlightened views which marked a good citizen. His outlook is clearly expressed in his essay on Isocrates in a passage which strikes the reader as a direct challenge to the Epicurean school: "Isocrates would make those who paid attention to him not merely clever speakers, but also good characters, serviceable to their family, their city, and the whole of Hellas...and if a man practises the genuine philosophy, *having regard not merely to its theoretical but to its practical side, and considering not how he may himself spend a life of tranquillity, but how he may benefit many besides himself*, then I would advise him to adopt the point of view of Isocrates."[3] It is to this end that Dionysius urges the need of a broad general education, in words which strongly recall the doctrines of Isocrates: "In short, who will not admit that it is essential for those who practise philosophic rhetoric to have studied the customs of many nations, both

---

[1] Cf. Egger, *op. cit.* p. 24.

[2] Egger, *op. cit.* pp. 23–4, and Hubbell, *loc. cit.* rightly stress the similarity of Dionysius' outlook to that of Isocrates; though I incline to think that much of Isocrates' teaching had been, and was still being, relayed through other schools; cf. Lehnert in Bursian 248, p. 84, who suggests that Rhodes may have been the intermediary source.

[3] *De Isoc.* c. 4 (= 1, 60–1) ἐξ ὧν οὐ λέγειν δεινοὺς μόνον ἀπεργάσαιτ' ἂν τοὺς προσέχοντας αὐτῷ τὸν νοῦν, ἀλλὰ καὶ τὰ ἤθη σπουδαίους, οἴκῳ τε καὶ πόλει καὶ ὅλη τῇ Ἑλλάδι χρησίμους...καὶ εἴ τις ἐπιτηδεύει τὴν ἀληθινὴν φιλοσοφίαν, μὴ τὸ θεωρητικὸν αὐτῆς μόνον ἀγαπῶν ἀλλὰ καὶ τὸ πρακτικόν, μηδ' ἀφ' ὧν αὐτὸς ἄλυπον ἕξει βίον, ταῦτα προαιρούμενος, ἀλλ' ἐξ ὧν πολλοὺς ὠφελήσει, παρακελευσαίμην ἂν αὐτῷ τὴν ἐκείνου τοῦ ῥήτορος μιμεῖσθαι προαίρεσιν. The contrast of πρακτικός and θεωρητικός is claimed as particularly Stoic by S. Striller, *De Stoicorum Studiis Rhetoricis* (Breslau, 1886), p. 29.

Greek and foreign, and to have heard about many laws and forms of government, the lives and actions of men, their deaths and their fortunes?"; and it is significant that the author recommended as valuable for such *encyclopädische Bildung* is Theopompus, "most famous of all the pupils of Isocrates" (*Ep. ad Pomp.* c. 6 = 11, 245).

With this desire to be of service to the state as his major aim, Dionysius contemplated the condition of the eloquence of his contemporaries, and found therein much to praise but still something of which to disapprove. There still lingered, he tells us,[1] some of the vices of "Asiatic" oratory, against which the previous generation had seen so strong a reaction. Wherever this reaction had started,[2] whether it was originally due to the teaching of the Rhodian school, or to the scholars of Alexandria, or to the doctrines of the Stoics of Pergamum, or to the study of classical Greek literature at Athens, it had reached its culminating point in the years between 55 and 46 B.C. In the *De Oratore* of Cicero there is little or no trace of it;[3] but the *Brutus* and *Orator* are both strongly imbued with the spirit of this literary polemic. As was only to be expected, the revulsion of feeling which had resulted from the excesses of the so-called "Asianism" had led to the cultivation of a style marked by chastened simplicity and extreme correctness, and Lysias and other exponents of the plain style had in Cicero's day become the sole models of Brutus, Calvus, Calidius, and others of the extremist set.[4] How misguided was such a view of style, and how unsatisfactory so limited a choice of models, Cicero clearly saw, and strove to correct the extremist tendency, particularly by stressing the necessity for a wider conception of the virtue of style,[5] and by advocating the choice of Demosthenes as a model.[6] When therefore Dionysius and Caecilius in the Augustan Age came to express their views on the controversy they found that the pendulum

---

[1] *Proem. init.*

[2] For the literature of this much-vexed question see especially H. Heck, *Zur Entstehung des rhetorischen Attizismus* (Munich, 1917), pp. 5–8, and cf. more recently, D'Alton, *Roman Literary Theory and Criticism* (London, 1931), pp. 215 ff.

[3] D'Alton, *op. cit.* pp. 224 ff. finds slight indications.

[4] *Orator*, §§ 28 ff.; *Brutus*, § 64, etc.   [5] *Orator*, §§ 100 ff.

[6] *Orator*, §§ 110 ff.; *Brutus*, §§ 35, 288; *De Opt. Gen. Or.* § 13.

had swung to a more settled position. Assuredly the death-blow to
Asianism still remained to be dealt, but there was also work of a
more positive nature to be done; and this lay in recalling their contemporaries to the study, not of one particular style or author, but
of all the great prose-writers of classical Greece. Hence arose the
need for a fuller treatment of the Greek orators in particular, which
the essays of Dionysius and the treatise of Caecilius, Περὶ τοῦ
χαρακτῆρος τῶν δέκα ῥητόρων, supplied. "Vos exemplaria Graeca
nocturna versate manu versate diurna" became the watchword of
Dionysius and Caecilius in prose, as of Horace in poetry. So the
principle of μίμησις, long firmly entrenched iń the rhetorical schools,
received a new lease of life, and was strongly emphasised by Dionysius in his efforts to re-establish a healthy prose style.

It becomes, therefore, a matter of the greatest importance to stress
the fact that Dionysius was led to literary criticism by practical and
utilitarian considerations, not by any strong urge to express in
words the effect upon himself of the masterpieces of Greek prose.
If then in his work we miss that personal enthusiasm and whole-
hearted admiration which pervade the celebrated treatise of
"Longinus", and find in its place steady, systematic analysis and
judicious weighing-up of merits and defects, we shall attribute this
not merely to the difference of personal character and outlook, but
also to the difference in the *aims* of the two critics. The author of
the Περὶ Ὕψους had before him a subject which allowed him all the
freedom and opportunity for self-expression that a critic could wish;
Dionysius set before himself a task that demanded constant research,
and considered it his duty to perform a service to eloquence in his
own age, not to create a treasure of literature that should live for
ever.

When he began, Dionysius had before him the accumulated mass
of Greek literature; it was clearly necessary for him to exercise
discrimination and to select representatives of oratory, history, and
poetry who seemed most deserving of careful study. Herein, of
course, he had the advantage of being able to examine the lists or
"canons" of the Alexandrian and Pergamene scholars who had
preceded him. It is noteworthy, however, that Dionysius did not
always accept the opinions of others; for he pays no attention
whatever to the canon of the orators, employed by Caecilius as the

basis of his work on the orators, but makes his own selection. The chief authors upon whose work he makes some critical comment are as follows: Homer, Hesiod, Antimachus, Panyasis, Simonides, Stesichorus, Sappho, Alcaeus, Pindar, Aeschylus, Sophocles, Euripides, Menander; Herodotus, Thucydides, Philistus, Xenophon, Theopompus; Gorgias, Thrasymachus, Lysias, Isocrates, Isaeus, Demosthenes, Aeschines, Hyperides, Lycurgus, and Dinarchus. However much his remarks on these authors may vary in length and in value, it cannot be denied that Dionysius hereby produced more actual criticism of Greek literature than any other writer whose works have survived. It is, therefore, of particular interest to study the methods which he employed, and to set forth his ideas of good and bad in literature when he approached his task.

It was almost unavoidable that a writer whose *alma mater* had been the rhetorical school should be deeply influenced by those traditional doctrines of "virtues" and "vices" of style which had been evolved by generations of scholars from the time of Aristotle himself. Dionysius did not, and indeed could not, at first exercise an absolutely independent mind in deciding what was praiseworthy and what was culpable in style; tradition had supplied him with a system, ready-made, perfected to the last detail, the composite result of the thought of countless predecessors; and if he began by applying this system to the criticism of literature, he was merely taking the line of least resistance and doing what any other rhetorician would have done in his place.

It will be to the purpose therefore to trace very briefly the history of the virtues of style, which formed the backbone of the system used by Dionysius.

In the third book of his *Rhetoric* Aristotle had made no mention of virtues of style; for him, style had one ἀρετή, and one only, and that was lucidity; speech must be clear in order to fulfil its proper function.[1] But he hastened to stress in addition to this primary

---

[1] *Rhet.* III, 2, § 1. Cope-Sandys *ad loc.* wrongly translate ἀρετή as "*one* virtue", implying that Aristotle recognised more than one. But cf. § 6 (αὕτη [*sc.* τὸ σαφηνίζειν] δ' ἦν ἡ τοῦ ῥητορικοῦ λόγου ἀρετή) and see the sound remarks of Hendrickson, "The Peripatetic Mean of Style and the Three Stylistic Characters" (*A.J.P.* xxv [1904], pp. 125-46) and Stroux, *De Theophrasti virtutibus dicendi* (Leipzig, 1912), pp. 30-1.

requirement the need for appropriateness (to speaker and occasion), since style could be clear and yet bare, or clear and yet unduly high-flown. His full definition therefore, framed in accordance with his celebrated doctrine of the Mean,[1] was: ὡρίσθω λέξεως ἀρετὴ σαφῆ εἶναι...καὶ μήτε ταπεινὴν μήτε ὑπὲρ τὸ ἀξίωμα, ἀλλὰ πρέπουσαν. This Mean, he argued, could only be preserved by introducing into one's style some element of distinction, such as would be imparted by a judicious use of metaphor; and this element of distinction would have the additional value of attracting the listeners' attention.[2] Throughout the book Aristotle insists on this principle of clearness governed by propriety, and leaves the subject of style with a final remark on the futility of further subdivision, and the superfluity of the demand that style should be pleasant and magnificent.[3] This parting shot was in all probability aimed at Theodectes,[4] and shows quite clearly that a double or even triple division[5] existed in Aristotle's own day.

Although Aristotle had insisted on the essential unity of his principle, his pupil and successor Theophrastus appears to have arrived at a fourfold division by analysing closely his master's typically concentrated thought. There is very strong evidence[6] for believing that in his Περὶ Λέξεως, unhappily long since lost, Theophrastus considered the virtues of style to be (1) purity of

[1] Cf. Hendrickson, *op. cit.*

[2] *Rhet.* III, 2, § 3 διὸ δεῖ ποιεῖν ξένην τὴν διάλεκτον· θαυμασταὶ γὰρ τῶν ἀπόντων εἰσίν, ἡδὺ δὲ τὸ θαυμαστόν, and § 8 καὶ τὸ σαφὲς καὶ τὸ ἡδὺ καὶ τὸ ξενικὸν ἔχει μάλιστα ἡ μεταφορά.

[3] *Ib.* 12, § 6 τὸ δὲ προσδιαιρεῖσθαι τὴν λέξιν, ὅτι ἡδεῖαν δεῖ καὶ μεγαλο-πρεπῆ, περίεργον.

[4] Cf. Quintilian IV, 2, 63: "Theodectes...non magnificam modo vult esse, verum etiam iucundam expositionem". (Theodectes is speaking of the style of narrative, not of style in general.)

[5] According as we regard ἡδὺ καὶ μεγαλοπρεπές as one or two virtues; Stroux, *op. cit.* pp. 39–40, contends that it represents a single idea of "ornateness", like Cicero's "ornatum illud, suave et adfluens" (*Orator*, § 79).

[6] See the full exposition of Stroux (*op. cit.* pp. 9–28), who bases his reconstruction of Theophrastus' doctrine on Cicero, *Orator*, § 79, and *De Oratore* III, 37, and Porphyrius *apud* Simplic. *in* Aristot. Categ. (ed. Kalbfleisch, p. 10).

language (ἑλληνισμός), (2) lucidity (σαφήνεια), (3) appropriateness (τὸ πρέπον), and (4) ornament (κατασκευή). Theophrastus thereby did little more than tabulate Aristotle's ideas, his first virtue being merely a more emphatic reproduction of Aristotle's insistence, in c. 5 of his work, on correctness in forms, terminations, and connections, his second and third virtues being due to a division of what Aristotle meant to be a single idea, clearness governed by propriety, and his final virtue being Aristotle's requirement for an element of distinction (τὸ ξενικόν), in a new dress.[1]

The impulse was thus given to further subdivision, and the process, once begun, knew no limit;[2] it was taken one stage farther by the Stoic theorist, Diogenes of Babylon,[3] who raised the number of virtues to five by the inclusion of brevity (συντομία); his other four virtues were those of Theophrastus.[4] As Diogenes was an influential teacher, it may be assumed that his five-fold division became part of the accepted stylistic doctrine of the Stoic school.

The Stoic division, however, was not accepted by Cicero, who is our only authority[5] on virtues of style during the period between Diogenes of Babylon and Dionysius; for he expressly excludes[6] the virtue of brevity, which the Stoics had added. Instead, he retains, as his virtues, purity of language, lucidity, propriety, and ornament,[7] and it is presumably to these that he alludes when he

---

[1] Cf. Mayer, *Theophrasti περὶ λέξεως libri fragmenta (cum prolegg.)* [Leipzig, 1910], pp. xv and xviii; Stroux, *op. cit.* p. 34, corrects Mayer at several points, but agrees that the fundamental ideas are in Aristotle.

[2] It is interesting to compare the gradual increase made by succeeding theorists in the number of the parts of speech, recorded by Dionysius, *De Comp. Verb.* c. 2 (= 11, 6 ff., and Roberts' edition, pp. 70 ff.).

[3] *Apud* Diog. Laert. VII, 59 ἀρεταὶ δὲ λόγου εἰσὶ πέντε· Ἑλληνισμός, σαφήνεια, συντομία, πρέπον, κατασκευή κ.τ.λ.

[4] Some doubt has arisen over the meaning attached by the Stoics to κατασκευή; but see Stroux, pp. 35–6.

[5] *Auctor ad Herennium* nowhere specifically mentions virtues of style; Stroux, p. 65, endeavours to extract them from IV, 12, 17 (cf. D'Alton, *op. cit.* p. 77, n. 5).

[6] *Brutus,* § 50: "brevitas autem laus est interdum in aliqua parte dicendi, in universa eloquentia laudem non habet"—i.e. Cicero agrees with theorists who relegate brevity to the διήγησις; cf. Kroll on *Orator,* § 139.

[7] *De Oratore* I, 144, III, 37; *Orator,* § 79.

2

claims that "omnes oratoriae virtutes" are to be found in the speeches of Cato.[1]

It is nevertheless probable that, even before Cicero wrote, more than one ingenious theorist had been at work adding to the ever-growing list of virtues of style, for we find that the stylistic system employed by Dionysius contains more than double the number of virtues found in any previous writer. That this development is not entirely the innovation of Dionysius is suggested by his remark[2] that the whole subject of virtues of style had before his time received the most detailed treatment. The process of subdivision, though natural in its origin, as indicating a desire to examine more closely the qualities which went to make a beautiful or striking style, had degenerated into the production of a mere list of possible attributes; the distinction between each separate virtue had become finer and finer, and there was now danger of wholeness and soundness of view being lost in the maze of terminological intricacies. Moreover, virtues which to the earlier philosophers had been merely dis-coverable elements in a good style had become in the eyes of rhetoricians essential demands. It was therefore fatally easy for any would-be critic to count the number of virtues instead of assessing their quality and appeal,[3] and to lose that power of indi-vidual thought and expression which is, in our view, so essential a requisite for his task.

The system of virtues which Dionysius employed[4] is fully set out in the excerpt from his work on imitation which is contained in the

[1] *Brutus*, § 65.

[2] *De Thuc.* c. 22 (= I, 358) καὶ γὰρ ταῦτα τῆς ἀκριβεστάτης τέτευχεν ἐξεργασίας. Cf. also *Ep. ad Pomp.* c. 3 (= II, 239) ἐνάργεια μετὰ ταῦτα τέτακται.

[3] Cf. [Longinus] Π. Ὕψ. c. 33, 1 καὶ ἔτι νὴ Δία πότερόν ποτε αἱ πλείους ἀρεταὶ τὸ πρωτεῖον ἐν λόγοις ἢ αἱ μείζους δικαίως ἂν φέροιντο;

[4] See the following: G. Ammon, *De D.H. Librorum Rhetoricorum Fontibus* (Munich, 1889), pp. 62–6; W. R. Roberts, *D.H., The Three Literary Letters*, p. 172; E. Kremer, *Über das rhetorische System des Dionys von Halikarnass* (Strassburg, 1907), pp. 45 ff.; and especially P. Geigenmüller, *Quaestiones Dionysianae de vocabulis artis criticae* (Leipzig, 1908), pp. 1–71; Stroux, *op. cit.* pp. 72 ff.; J. D. Meerwaldt, *De Dionysiana virtutum et generum dicendi doctrina* (= *Studia ad generum dicendi historiam pertinentia*, I) (Amsterdam, 1920), pp. 1–26.

epistle to Pompeius Geminus (c. 3). It is evident from a comparison with Dionysius' remarks in *De Thucydide*, c. 22, that the list of virtues is here divided into those which are "essential" (ἀναγκαῖαι) and those which are chiefly ornamental or "additional" (ἐπίθετοι). Under the former heading come (1) Purity of language (τὸ καθαρόν), (2) Lucidity (σαφήνεια), (3) Brevity (συντομία). Under the latter he includes a great number of virtues, which fall into the following groups:[1] (1) Vividness (ἐνάργεια), (2) Power of character-drawing and emotional representation (ἡ τῶν ἠθῶν τε καὶ παθῶν μίμησις), (3) Grandeur, impressiveness (τὸ μέγα καὶ θαυμαστόν, etc.), (4) Vigour, power (ἰσχύς, τόνος, etc.), (5) Charm, persuasiveness (ἡδονή, πειθώ, etc.), (6) Propriety (τὸ πρέπον). Dionysius does not tell us in this passage of the Περὶ Μιμήσεως what are the relative values of these two groups, but his views in the matter can easily be gathered from other remarks in the essays.[2] "Essential" virtues are directed towards a clear and intelligible exposition, and as a result are to be demanded of every writer. "Additional" virtues impart to style beauty, vigour, and magnificence; they serve to reveal the rhetorician's power. To lack an "additional" virtue, therefore, is merely to betray a weakness: to lack an "essential" virtue is to commit an unpardonable offence.

This twofold grouping of virtues of style may at first sight appear to be an innovation of Dionysius, especially as it is not found in any earlier Greek rhetorician; but Dionysius himself includes it in his sketch of the stylistic system in *De Thucydide*, c. 22, with the words εἴρηται πολλοῖς πρότερον, and there are indications of it in Cicero.[3]

[1] Geigenmüller, *op. cit.* (p. 34) groups the ἀρεταὶ ἐπίθετοι differently, but his classification has not been followed by Stroux (p. 77, n. 1) and Meerwaldt (p. 15, n. 3).

[2] Esp. *De Dem.* c. 18 (= I, 165–6) καθαρεύει τε γὰρ εἴ τις ἄλλη τοῖς ὀνόμασι καὶ τὴν διάλεκτόν ἐστιν ἀκριβής, φανερά τ' ἐστὶ καὶ κοινὴ καὶ τὰς ἄλλας ἀρετὰς ἁπάσας περιείληφεν, ἐξ ὧν ἂν μάλιστα γένοιτο διάλεκτος σαφής, and *De Thuc.* c. 23 (= I, 360) τὰς μὲν οὖν ἀναγκαίας ἀρετὰς ἡ λέξις αὐτῶν πάντων ἔχει (καὶ γὰρ καθαρὰ καὶ σαφὴς καὶ σύντομός ἐστιν ἀποχρώντως, σῴζουσα τὸν ἴδιον ἑκάστη τῆς διαλέκτου χαρακτῆρα)· τὰς δ' ἐπιθέτους, ἐξ ὧν μάλιστα διάδηλος ἡ τοῦ ῥήτορος γίνεται δύναμις, οὔτε ἁπάσας οὔτε εἰς ἄκρον ἠκούσας κ.τ.λ.

[3] *Part. Or.* § 31, *Brutus*, § 261, *De Orat.* III, 52; cf. Geigenmüller, *op. cit.* p. 12.

The treatise, therefore, which first included this division may have appeared at any time between the third and the first century B.C. But although the origin of the division cannot be determined, Dionysius' remarks on the two types of virtues enable us to see it in an interesting historical perspective. Aristotle's single virtue of τὸ σαφές had not satisfied Theophrastus, who had added correctness, and made this equally indispensable; the Stoics had then added brevity. Correctness, lucidity, brevity—these became the essential virtues of Dionysius, but it is interesting to note that he refers to them in *De Dem.* c. 18, as ἀρετάς, ἐξ ὧν ἂν μάλιστα γένοιτο διά-λεκτος σαφής: for this very clearly shows that Aristotle's was still the predominant influence, and that Dionysius was conscious of the fact that intervening theorists had really only elaborated Aristotle's doctrine of lucidity. The "essential" virtues thus represent the primary demand of the philosopher—that language shall in the first instance perform its duty of explaining the facts.

Light is also thrown on the origin of the "additional" virtues by the remark of Dionysius (*De Thuc.* c. 23) that it is these ἐξ ὧν μάλιστα διάδηλος ἡ τοῦ ῥήτορος γίνεται δύναμις; for it must have been in the rhetorical schools that such virtues as he includes in this category were particularly encouraged. Had Aristotle not been considering style from the point of view of its value to a public speaker, he would hardly have troubled to qualify his one demand that it should be clear. But he did qualify that demand by adding that an element of distinction was necessary in order to capture the attention of the audience. This was a concession to rhetoric, and it is in this demand for an element of distinction in style, for devices which will affect the hearer besides explaining the case, that the germ of the "additional" virtues of Dionysius is to be found. This concession appears in Theophrastus as a full virtue, κατασκευή, and even has a place in the Stoic doctrine; though, owing to their parti-cular insistence on a plain style, κατασκευή was rigidly limited by the Stoics to λέξις ἐκπεφευγυῖα τὸν ἰδιωτισμόν. In Cicero, however, κατασκευή appears in the guise of ornament, which takes a much more important place and is responsible for imparting to style pleasantness (*suavitas, delectare*), and power (*vis, movere*). The conclusion, therefore, is not unwarranted that the "additional" virtues of Dionysius had their origin in the demands of teachers in the rhetorical schools at a very early date for something more than correctness and lucidity.[1] In short, the whole system, as Dionysius inherited it, may well be considered as a compromise in the age-old quarrel of philosopher and rhetorician.

Dionysius inherited more, however, than a system of virtues; this was only part of the elaborate stylistic doctrine which lay to his hand. An old tradition, dating back to Theophrastus,[2] taught him that in assessing the striking quality of any style (τὸ μέγα καὶ σεμνὸν καὶ περιττὸν ἐν λέξει) he must consider, first, choice of words (ἐκλογὴ τῶν ὀνομάτων); secondly, composition (ἁρμονία); and finally, use of figures (σχήματα). This traditional division, together with the various subdivisions which had subsequently been made within it, Dionysius applied to the criticism of style in general. An author's vocabulary would first be labelled as consisting of either ordinary, current words (κυρία φράσις), or figurative ones (τροπικὴ φράσις),[3] or a mixture of the two. Next his σύνθεσις would be examined; his phrases (κόμματα), his clauses (κῶλα), and his periods (περίοδοι) would be in turn considered,[4] and unless he merely strove to appear unaffected in composition (ἀφελὴς καὶ ἀνεπιτηδευτὸς σύνθεσις) he would be put into one of three types, "harsh", "smooth", or "mixed" (αὐστηρά, γλαφυρά, and μέση σύνθεσις).[5] Finally, his σχήματα would be studied and divided into those of single words (σχήματα ἁπλῶν ὀνομάτων—i.e. metaphors—this would to some extent overlap with the study of ἐκλογή), and those of words in combination (σχήματα συνθέτων ὀνομάτων).[6] It was by careful analysis in each of these three branches that the critic would gain a thorough insight into his author's style; here again traditional doctrine supplied the methods by which the investigation should be conducted.

Having ascertained the ἐκλογή, σύνθεσις, and σχήματα of an author and thereby gained assistance in arriving at the ἀρεταί, Dionysius (or any other user of the system) could then proceed farther along the

[1] D'Alton, *op. cit.* p. 77, remarks that "almost all his (Dionysius') 'superadded' virtues can be reduced to either Decorum or ornateness". I would argue that all, with the exception of τὸ πρέπον, are to be reduced to "ornateness".

[2] *De Isoc.* c. 3 *init.* (= 1, 58). Cf. *Auctor ad Herennium*, IV, 12, 17.

[3] Cf. *De Thuc.* c. 22 (= 1, 358).　　　　　　[4] *Ib.*

[5] *De Comp. Verb.* cc. 22–4; but see p. 24, n. 1.　　[6] *De Thuc.*, *loc. cit.*

rhetorical groove by placing his author in one of three general categories (χαρακτῆρες), the Plain, the Middle, or the Grand Style (λιτός, μέσος, ὑψηλός χαρακτήρ). Sometimes this procedure would work out with perfect smoothness. The author under consideration might be found to employ only ordinary words, authenticated by common usage (κύρια καὶ κοινὰ ὀνόματα), avoiding all that was strange (ξένα), poetical (ποιητικά), or archaic (ἀπηρχαιωμένα), and being very sparing in his use of metaphor (τροπικὴ φράσις). His composition, when examined, might also be found to carry out the same principle of adherence to the spoken language, simplicity and naturalness being its keynotes (ἀφελὴς σύνθεσις). Finally embellishments, such as result from the use of figures, might well be entirely absent. The virtues which would result in this kind of style would be likely to be purity of language, and lucidity, and possibly brevity; but few of the "additional" virtues would be found, owing to the self-imposed limitation in the author's choice of words, composition, and figures. It would be obvious to the user of the system that the writer under consideration belonged to a very definite type, the exponents of the Plain Style, and nothing would be easier, and indeed nothing more justifiable, than to enclose him for ever within that category. Or again, the very opposite might happen, and a writer whose vocabulary was freely decorated with poetical, rare, and strange words, whose composition appeared deliberately abnormal, whose employment of the external ornaments of style was unlimited, would abound in those additional virtues of which every rhetorician was proud, and even perhaps go so far in his temerity as to risk the sacrifice of one of the essential virtues. Clearly he would be marked down for the Grand Style.

But sometimes, and, in fact, often, the system would not function so well. If an author's style, ever an individual and often an elusive thing, could not be pinned down as Plain or Grand, there was no alternative but to relegate it to the Middle; and as a result the Middle category was the only home for a very oddly assorted company.[1] The characteristics of the Middle Style became hard to define; and even supposing them to have been settled, there was always the difficulty of deciding exactly where one type ended and another began.

[1] Cf. D'Alton, op. cit. p. 73.

Such was the system which was bequeathed to the critic Dionysius, a system so rigorously defined that it may be set out in tabular form (see overleaf). To what extent it had been put to the use of literary criticism before Dionysius wrote, it is difficult to say. Cicero occasionally applies part of the system to criticism; when, for instance, he says of Antonius:[1] "in verbis et eligendis...et conlocandis...nihil non ad rationem et tamquam ad artem dirigebat; verum multo magis hoc idem in sententiarum ornamentis et conformationibus", he is clearly criticising according to the division ἐκλογή, σύνθεσις, and σχήματα.[2] Similarly his remark that readers of Cato's speeches should select striking and praiseworthy passages since "all the oratorical virtues will be found in them"[3] suggests that already the system was being brought into relation with literary texts for purposes of criticism. But there is no indication of any specific work of this kind before Dionysius; and there does not seem any valid reason for refusing to accept Dionysius' well-known claim to originality[4] in the sense that he was the first to apply the traditional system to criticism of separate authors in essays expressly designed to serve the practical purpose of μίμησις. The faults which use of the system was likely to produce are obvious, and there is no need to stress its cramping influence. Nor would a study which aimed solely at illustrating the hampering effect of rhetoric upon the criticism of Dionysius in any way do justice to him as a critic. It is the purpose of the present work to examine carefully the methods which Dionysius employs in each essay in turn, to consider how far he freed himself from the shackles of the rhetorical system, and, particularly, to decide whether or not there is a gradual improvement in his powers of critical exposition. Before this question can be settled, it is first of all necessary to assess, as far as possible, the order of composition of Dionysius' critical works—a study which in itself would be but a barren academical exercise, but which, when made ancillary to the purpose of illustrating mental development, may serve to help the reader to form a truer estimate of Dionysius as a literary critic.

[1] *Brutus,* § 140.
[2] With the one difference that Cicero speaks of σχήματα διανοίας, not σχήματα λέξεως.
[3] *Brutus,* § 65.   [4] *Praef.* c. 4 (= I, 7).

THE STYLISTIC SYSTEM OF DIONYSIUS

Choice of words (ἐκλογὴ τῶν ὀνομάτων)	Composition¹ (σύνθεσις τῶν ὀνομάτων)	Figures (σχήματα λέξεως)	Virtues and failings (ἀρεταὶ καὶ κακίαι λέξεως)	Types of style (χαρακτῆρες λέξεως)
Common words in everyday use (κοινά, κύρια ὀνόματα, κυρία λέξις, συνήθης διάλεκτος, etc.)	Apparently artless; like that of the average individual (ἀφελὴς καὶ ἀνεπιτήδευτος)	Not introduced; no embellishment (& ἀκόσμητος)	Essential virtues: purity, accuracy, lucidity, brevity. Additional virtues rare. Failing: lack of power	Plain (λιτός)
Common words in everyday use, with occasional metaphors	Smooth, harmonious, rhythmical (γλαφυρά, εὔρυθμος)	Parallelisms, antitheses, etc. (παρίσωσις, παρομοίωσις, ἀντίθεσις)	Essential virtues: purity, accuracy, lucidity. Additional virtues: pleasantness, stateliness, etc. Failings: lack of brevity, vigour, etc.	Middle (μέσος, μικτός)
Poetical, rare, strange, archaic, and metaphorical words frequently used (ποιητικὰ ὀνόματα, γλῶτται, ξένα ὀνόματα, etc.)	Rough and severe, no heed being paid to euphony (αὐστηρά)	Frequent figures (λέξις ἐγκατάσκευος, περιττή, τοῖς ἐπιθέτοις κόσμοις συμπεπληρωμένη)	Additional virtues: power, weight, vigour, appeal, magnificence, etc. Possible lack of purity, lucidity and brevity	Grand (ὑψηλός)

¹ The three types of composition named in *De Comp. Verb.* viz. αὐστηρά, γλαφυρά, and μέση σύνθεσις, do not exactly fit this scheme, and I believe them to represent a later development made by Dionysius himself. It is noticeable that the ἀφελὴς σύνθεσις, frequently mentioned elsewhere, does not appear in the types given in *De Comp. Verb.*

CHAPTER II

The order of composition of the Scripta Rhetorica[1]

THERE can, unfortunately, be no absolute certainty about the order in which Dionysius produced his literary essays. There is no dearth of evidence, for Dionysius quite frequently refers his readers to some previous work on a particular author or point of criticism, and also frequently promises to elucidate his statements more fully in a later study. But these references cannot always be identified; and identification is sometimes made more difficult by the fact that Dionysius composed several works on an author such as Demosthenes, so that a vague phrase such as τὴν περὶ Δημο-σθένους πραγματείαν[2] or ἐν τοῖς περὶ Δημοσθένους[3] does not enable the reader to say exactly where the reference belongs. When the evidence of direct reference is exhausted, it is only possible to make deductions from the general form of the essays, from the knowledge of other extant essays which they may seem to presuppose in the reader, or from omissions which may be regarded as significant. It is only with caution that such supplementary evidence may be used; but taken together with the references of Dionysius himself, it helps towards the formulation of an order of composition which may claim to be, at least, strongly probable.

[1] See A. G. Becker, *Dionysius von Halikarnassos über die Rednergewalt des Demosthenes vermittelst seiner Schreibart* (Leipzig, 1829), *praef.* pp. xl–xlvii; C. J. Weismann, *De D.H. vita et scriptis* (Göttingen, 1837); F. Blass, *De D.H. Scriptis Rhetoricis* (Bonn, 1863); C. T. Roessler, *D.H. Scriptorum Rhetoricorum Fragmenta* (Leipzig, 1873), pp. 1–13; H. Rabe, *Rhein. Mus. N.F.* XLVIII (1893), pp. 147–51; U. von Wilamowitz-Möllendorff, *Hermes*, XXXIV (1899), pp. 625–7; H. Usener, *Praef.* XXXIV; W. R. Roberts, *D.H., The Three Literary Letters*, pp. 4–7; M. Egger, *Denys d'Halicarnasse* (Paris, 1902), pp. 29–33; R. H. Tukey, *Classical Philology*, IV (1909), pp. 390–404, and *Classical Review*, XXIII (1909), p. 188; E. Kalinka, *Wiener Studien*, XLIII (1922–3), pp. 157–68, and XLIV (1924–5), pp. 48–68. I regret that the first two have been inaccessible, and are known to me only through Blass, *op. cit.*

[2] *De Thuc.* c. 1 (= 1, 326).

[3] *De Dinarcho*, c. 11 (= 1, 313); cf. *De Dem.* c. 57 *sub fin.* (= 1, 251).

It is natural to take as starting point the plan of work which Dionysius sets forth in the preface to his treatise on the orators, for his intentions are there stated without ambiguity. He declares that he intends to treat those orators whom he has selected as the finest models[1] in two separate volumes (συντάξεις), of which the first is to contain studies of the older orators, Lysias, Isocrates, and Isaeus, and the second studies of the younger orators, Demosthenes, Hyperides, and Aeschines.[2] He also expresses the intention of studying the historians later.[3] It has been well observed[4] that, when Dionysius wrote this Preface, he had already written the first of the two volumes, for he says: τὴν δὲ ἀρχὴν ἀπὸ ταύτης λήψεται (sc. ἡ πραγματεία) τῆς ὑπὲρ τῶν πρεσβυτέρων γραφείσης; so that there is at least a *prima facie* case for supposing the essays on Lysias, Isocrates, and Isaeus to have been composed in the order in which Dionysius mentioned them and in which they now stand in our text. This assumption is in part justified by the concluding words of the *De Lysia*, which prove that Dionysius proceeded at once from Lysias to Isocrates.[5] The concluding words of the *De Isocrate* do not contain any reference to an immediate transition to Isaeus, but there does not seem to be any compelling reason why Dionysius should at that point have directed his attention to another study. It has, however, been argued[6] that whereas in the *De Isaeo* the importance of Isaeus as a precursor of Demosthenes is fully recognised, he is mentioned in the *De Demosthene* (c. 8) as among those who οὐθὲν οὔτε καινὸν οὔτε περιττὸν ἐπετήδευσαν; and the conclusion has accordingly been drawn that Dionysius could hardly have produced

---

[1] *Praef.* c. 4 (= I, 7) τοὺς δὲ χαριεστάτους ἐξ αὐτῶν προχειρισάμενος κ.τ.λ.

[2] *Ib.* ἔσονται δὲ οἱ παραλαμβανόμενοι ῥήτορες τρεῖς μὲν ἐκ τῶν πρεσβυτέρων, Λυσίας Ἰσοκράτης Ἰσαῖος, τρεῖς δ' ἐκ τῶν ἐπακμασάντων τούτοις, Δημοσθένης Ὑπερείδης Αἰσχίνης...καὶ διαιρεθήσεται μὲν εἰς δύο συντάξεις ἡ πραγματεία, τὴν δὲ ἀρχὴν ἀπὸ ταύτης λήψεται τῆς ὑπὲρ τῶν πρεσβυτέρων γραφείσης.

[3] *Ib.* ἐὰν δὲ ἐγχωρῇ, καὶ περὶ τῶν ἱστορικῶν.

[4] By J. Stroux, *op. cit.* p. 112.

[5] *De Lys.* c. 34 (= I, 53) ἕπεται δὲ τῷ ῥήτορι τούτῳ (sc. τῷ Λυσίᾳ) κατὰ τὴν τάξιν τῶν χρόνων Ἰσοκράτης. περὶ δὴ τούτου λεκτέον ἐφεξῆς ἑτέραν ἀρχὴν λαβοῦσιν.

[6] By Kalinka, *op. cit.* pp. 163-4.

a special essay on Isaeus when he made this remark. Yet this argument is unconvincing; for Dionysius in the passage quoted, as the context clearly shows, merely means that Isaeus was not, like Lysias, Isocrates, and Thucydides, an example of a particularly individual type of style;[1] this does not deny all importance to Isaeus,[2] and is in fact no more than Dionysius had said in the *De Isaeo* where he had apologized for introducing a special study of Isaeus, since he showed so much similarity to Lysias in style.[3] Moreover, the first twelve chapters of the *De Isaeo* have an unmistakable connection with the *De Lysia;* for throughout these chapters Dionysius contrasts Isaeus with Lysias. The essay in fact constantly looks back on the *De Lysia* in this respect. Not until chapter thirteen of the *De Isaeo* does Dionysius turn to consider the influence of Isaeus on Demosthenes; and there would be no point whatever in the first twelve chapters if, as has been suggested,[4] Dionysius wrote the essay on Isaeus when already in the middle of the *De Demosthene.* Such an argument merely introduces unnecessary complications, and gives no reason whatsoever why Dionysius should have suddenly turned to produce a special essay on Isaeus, full of comparisons between him and Lysias, in the middle of an essay devoted to Demosthenes.

The question of the composition of the second σύνταξις of the

---

[1] I agree entirely with Tukey, *op. cit.* p. 398 "The expression... is not to be taken absolutely, but is to be interpreted in the light of the context and of the underlying purpose of the essay. So far as it was a question of the three styles without regard to their development, Isaeus presented nothing novel."

[2] Isaeus' influence is admittedly not given the prominence in *De Dem.* that it has in *De Isaeo* for the simple reason that in *De Dem.* Dionysius is not primarily considering the *influences* on Demosthenes' style, but is concerned to prove the superiority of Demosthenes to the accepted models of each *type* of style, and Isaeus did not represent any one specific type.

[3] c. 20 (= I, 123) τὸν δὲ δὴ τρίτον Ἰσαῖον εἴ τις ἔροιτό με τίνος ἕνεκα προσεθέμην, Λυσίου δὴ ζηλωτὴν ὄντα, ταύτην ἂν αὐτῷ φαίην τὴν αἰτίαν, ὅτι...κ.τ.λ.; cf. c. 2 (= I, 94). In view of these definite statements Dionysius' description of Isaeus in *De Dinarcho init.* as a εὑρετής must simply be regarded as an inconsistency.

[4] By Kalinka, pp. 163 ff. who puts the *De Isaeo* after *De Dem.* c. 32—a gratuitous assumption.

work on the orators is one which has caused a more real difficulty; for not only have the essays on Hyperides and Aeschines (if they were ever composed) entirely disappeared, but also the beginning of the extant essay on the style of Demosthenes, which would in all probability have contained valuable evidence, is lost. Moreover, there are certain differences of treatment in the extant *De Demosthene* which have led to the supposition that it does not belong to the treatise on the orators at all, but is a separate, independent production. However, before these deductions from the form of the *De Demosthene* are considered, it is necessary to present two pieces of fairly definite evidence given by the author himself. First, in c. 2 of the essay, Dionysius has an unmistakable reference to the first group of essays on the orators, and more particularly to the *De Lysia*, when he dismisses the idea of a lengthy study of Lysias with the words τίς δὲ ἦν ἡ προαίρεσις αὐτοῦ καὶ τίς ἡ δύναμις, ἐν τῇ πρὸ ταύτης δεδήλωται γραφῇ. Similarly, when he says of Isocrates, ὅντινα χαρακτῆρα ἔχειν ἐφαίνετό μοι, διὰ πλειόνων μὲν ἐδήλωσα πρότερον,[1] he is clearly referring his readers to the *De Isocrate*. In view of these statements and the arguments already adduced regarding the *De Isaeo*, it cannot be doubted that the *De Demosthene* was composed later than the *De Lysia*, *De Isocrate*, and *De Isaeo*. Indeed, the phrase τῇ πρὸ ταύτης γραφῇ is in itself almost enough to suggest that the first σύνταξις on the orators had not long preceded, and that the *De Demosthene* is in actual fact the beginning of the second σύνταξις. Such an interpretation finds strong support in the opening sentence of the second chapter of Dionysius' epistle to Pompeius (an epistle directly occasioned by the *De Demosthene*), in which Dionysius quotes a substantial passage of the *De Demosthene* with the words λοιπὸν δ' ἐστί μοι καὶ περὶ αὐτῶν ὧν εἴρηκα λόγων περὶ τἀνδρὸς ἐν τῇ περὶ τῶν 'Αττικῶν πραγματείᾳ ῥητόρων εἰπεῖν. These words, despite the alteration of ἀρχαίων to 'Αττικῶν, are most naturally taken as referring to the treatise of which the essays on Lysias, Isocrates and Isaeus formed the first part. There is therefore very good ground for believing that the *De Demosthene* was the first essay of the second σύνταξις; and objections drawn from the shape and apparent purpose of the essay, though they require

---

[1] *De Dem.* c. 4 (= 1, 135). As Kalinka, *op. cit.* pp. 166-7, demonstrates at length, what follows is simply summarised from *De Isocrate*.

to be met in themselves, must nevertheless be considered to have been raised in the face of quite direct evidence afforded by the author himself.

At first sight, it might easily appear that the *De Demosthene* represented a change in Dionysius' original plan because it is solely occupied with style, and pays no attention to the πραγματικὸς τόπος of Demosthenes; but it is sufficient to point to the concluding words of the essay, where Dionysius promises a special work on this subject,[1] to disprove such a conclusion and to show that the study of the author as a whole, even if considerably longer, yet would have corresponded in treatment to the earlier essays. A more serious objection, however, is taken to the tone of the essay which, it is argued, is one of polemic rather than exposition;[2] Dionysius' scathing comments on Plato and his eagerness to prove the complete pre-eminence of Demosthenes in every type of style are held to point to an independent origin, to an essay specially directed against those detractors of the master-orator who were to be found in the philosophical schools. But this view does not seem to take into account the fact that Dionysius was dealing here with his favourite model, an author who even before his time was regarded as the perfect orator;[3] his desire to prove Demosthenes superior to all other writers was natural when he was writing for the purpose of arousing the enthusiasm of his readers for the most versatile of all the orators. That his purpose was not originally one of polemic is clear from his own reply to Pompeius (c. 1), in which he disclaims any intention of belittling Plato by extolling the merits of Demosthenes; such controversy as there was on this point arose *after* the appearance of the essay, but can hardly be considered to have inspired it. Finally, it has been argued[4] that the essay on Demosthenes as we

---

[1] *De Dem.* c. 58 (= 1, 252) ἐὰν δὲ σῴζῃ τὸ δαιμόνιον ἡμᾶς, καὶ περὶ τῆς πραγματικῆς αὐτοῦ (*sc.* τοῦ Δημοσθένους) δεινότητος...ἐν τοῖς ἑξῆς γραφησομένοις ἀποδώσομέν σοι τὸν λόγον.

[2] This is the view put forward by Tukey, *op. cit.* pp. 390–8; see also Stroux, *op. cit.* pp. 113–14.

[3] Cicero, *Brutus*, § 35: "nam plane quidem perfectum et quoi nihil admodum desit Demosthenem facile dixeris". Cf. *Orator*, §§ 6 and 23, and Dionysius, *De Isaeo*, c. 20 (= 1, 123).

[4] Tukey, *op. cit.* pp. 391 ff.

have it does not correspond to the description of the second σύνταξις of the work on the orators given by Dionysius in the opening words of his essay on Dinarchus. There Dionysius says: περὶ Δεινάρχου τοῦ ῥήτορος οὐδὲν εἰρηκὼς ἐν τοῖς περὶ τῶν ἀρχαίων γραφεῖσιν διὰ τὸ μήτε εὑρετὴν ἰδίου γεγονέναι χαρακτῆρος τὸν ἄνδρα, ὥσπερ τὸν Λυσίαν καὶ τὸν Ἰσοκράτην καὶ τὸν Ἰσαῖον, μήτε τῶν εὑρημένων ἑτέροις τελειωτήν, ὥσπερ τὸν Δημοσθένη καὶ τὸν Αἰσχίνη καὶ ⟨τὸν⟩ Ὑπερείδην ἡμεῖς κρίνομεν...ἡγησάμην δεῖν μὴ παραλιπεῖν αὐτόν κ.τ.λ. It is deduced from this that, in the second σύνταξις, Dionysius set out to show that Demosthenes perfected the style of Isaeus, Aeschines that of Isocrates, and Hyperides that of Lysias. If, indeed, such an interpretation were justified, there would be great difficulty in accepting the extant De Demosthene as the first essay of that σύνταξις. But the interpretation is not justified; for it involves the quite unnecessary assumption that Dionysius means that each of the three later orators imitated only one style each; on the contrary, τῶν εὑρημένων ἑτέροις τελειωτήν is easily taken to mean that they each used the resources placed at their disposal by their predecessors—that is, employed any or every type of style in the formation of their own. That Dionysius did not regard any of them as the cultivator of a single style is clear from his remark at the end of the De Isaeo[1] where he distinctly praises all three because ἡ... τελειοτάτη ῥητορικὴ καὶ τὸ κράτος τῶν ἐναγωνίων λόγων ἐν τούτοις τοῖς ἀνδράσιν ἔοικεν εἶναι. In point of fact, the passage from De Dinarcho very strongly supports the assumption that the De Demosthene, which certainly reveals Demosthenes as τῶν εὑρημένων ἑτέροις τελειωτήν, was the first essay of the second σύνταξις. Whether the essays on Hyperides and Aeschines were written it is hard to say for certain; the reference already quoted cannot be regarded as decisive proof.[2] However, if Dionysius did fulfil his intention of treating them, he assuredly did not try to prove Hyperides the perfector of the plain style only,[3] for this would seriously conflict with his own statement in De Dem. c. 2 that

---

[1] c. 20 sub fin. (= I, 124).

[2] Blass, p. 11, Roessler, p. 8, Egger, p. 30, and Tukey, p. 391, believe that these essays were composed, but Wilamowitz, p. 625, Stroux, p. 112, and Kalinka, pp. 157 ff. take the opposite view.

[3] As Tukey, p. 392, would have us believe.

Lysias "perfected the plain style and brought it to the highest pitch of its individual excellence".[1] Nor did he set out to prove that Aeschines perfected the middle style,[2] for he says in *De Dem.* c. 3 that Isocrates very nearly perfected it himself.[3] In short, the elaborate hypothesis built up largely on a mistaken interpretation of the opening sentence of the *De Dinarcho*, which would have us believe that three whole essays on Demosthenes, Hyperides and Aeschines dropped out of circulation and that a special study on the style of Demosthenes which had been added to the collection later survives in our *De Demosthene*, has little or nothing to justify it.[4] Such differences as there are between the *De Lysia*, *De Isocrate*, and *De Isaeo* on the one hand, and the *De Demosthene* on the other, will find a more satisfactory explanation later; for the present it is sufficient to note that the *De Dem.* followed the essays on the earlier orators as the first essay of the second σύνταξις originally promised.

There are, in chapters 49 and 50 of the *De Demosthene*, two quite explicit references to the treatise *De Compositione Verborum*.[5] These references, however, only serve to prove that the *De Comp. Verb.* preceded these chapters, not that it necessarily preceded the whole essay, and certainly not that it necessarily preceded the *De Lysia*, *De Isocrate*, and *De Isaeo* as well. It is, indeed, only with difficulty that the *De Comp. Verb.* can be regarded as earlier than the *De Demosthene*, for in c. 18 of the *De Comp. Verb.* there is a quite distinct reference to Dionysius' criticisms of Plato made in cc. 5–7

---

[1] I, 130 ἐτελείωσε δ' αὐτὴν (*sc.* τὴν λιτὴν λέξιν) καὶ εἰς ἄκρον ἤγαγε τῆς ἰδίας ἀρετῆς Λυσίας ὁ Κεφάλου.

[2] Tukey, *loc. cit.*, admits a difficulty here.

[3] I, 132 οἱ δὲ ἐκδεξάμενοι καὶ ἀναθρέψαντες καὶ οὐ πολὺ ἀποσχόντες τοῦ τελειῶσαι ῥητόρων μὲν Ἰσοκράτης ὁ Ἀθηναῖος ἐγένετο κ.τ.λ.

[4] Kalinka, p. 160, also regards this theory as untenable. Cf. also Lehnert in Bursian's *Jahresbericht* 248 (1935), p. 87. Apart from the objections mentioned, there is a very serious difficulty for Tukey in the words ἐν τῇ πρὸ τούτων γραφῇ, which he has to make to refer to *six* essays (p. 403, n. 3)!

[5] I, 236 εἰ δέ τις ἀπαιτήσει καὶ ταῦτ' ἔτι μαθεῖν ὅπῃ ποτ' ἔχει, τοὺς ὑπομνηματισμοὺς ἡμῶν λαβών, οὓς περὶ τῆς συνθέσεως τῶν ὀνομάτων πεπραγματεύμεθα, πάντα ὅσα ποθεῖ τῶν ἐνθάδε παραλειπομένων εἴσεται and I, 239 τὰς δὲ περὶ τούτου τοῦ μέρους πίστεις ἐν τοῖς περὶ τῆς συνθέσεως γραφεῖσιν ἀποδεδωκὼς οὐκ ἀναγκαῖον ἡγοῦμαι κἀνταῦθα λέγειν.

of the *De Demosthene*.[1] Those who refuse to acknowledge that the reference is to these chapters are forced to suppose that Dionysius made the same criticisms of Plato in another work now lost—a supposition which has little or nothing in its favour. The only reasonable conclusion is therefore that the *De Comp. Verb.* was written at some point between c. 7 and c. 49 of the *De Demosthene*. There is good reason to believe that it was after writing c. 33 of the *De Demosthene* that Dionysius turned to write the *De Comp. Verb.*[2] This supposition has the advantage of strong arguments. In the first place Dionysius is clearly drawing to the conclusion of his study of the λέξις of Demosthenes in c. 33; the opening words of that chapter restate the whole purpose of his study[3] and are followed by a summary of his results; a similar summary is found in *De Lysia* c. 13, before the πραγματικὸς τόπος of this author is considered (cf. *De Isoc.* c. 11). Yet, instead of proceeding to his new topic, Dionysius gives a further summary of his views on the superiority of Demosthenes to other stylists in c. 34, ἵν᾽ εὐσύνοπτος μᾶλλον γένηται...ὁ λόγος, and then proceeds to the discussion of σύνθεσις. Secondly, he himself regards this part of his work (cc. 34 ff.) as a fresh start, for when he says in c. 46 (*sub fin.*) ἐπάνειμι δ᾽ οὖν ἐπὶ τὰ λοιπά, ὧν ἐν ἀρχῇ προὐθέμην ἐρεῖν, he is referring to the plan outlined in c. 36 *init.* There is strong ground, therefore, for believing that after c. 33 there was a distinct break in the composition of the essay; and as the second half of the essay, which deals with the σύνθεσις of Demosthenes, is so strikingly similar in treatment, and even phraseology,[4]

---

[1] II, 77 νῦν δὲ περὶ μὲν τὴν ἐκλογὴν ἔστιν ὅτε διαμαρτάνει, καὶ μάλιστα ἐν οἷς ἂν τὴν ὑψηλὴν καὶ περιττὴν καὶ ἐγκατάσκευον διώκῃ φράσιν, ὑπὲρ ὧν ἑτέρωθί μοι δηλοῦται σαφέστερον. Here δηλοῦται is to be taken as a strict present (cf. Kalinka, p. 51), not as a future (Roessler, p. 4, criticised by Blass, *Philologische Anzeiger* (1873), v, 353) or a perfect (Blass, *loc. cit.*, Tukey, p. 399, n. 6); H. Richards' conjecture δεδήλωται (*C.R.* XIX (1905), p. 253) is unnecessary.

[2] See Tukey, pp. 399 ff., who, however, takes the break to be after c. 32—with less reason, I think. The idea of supposing an interruption in the composition of the *De Dem.* had occurred to Blass (p. 9). Kalinka, p. 50, adopts Tukey's hypothesis.

[3] Cf. c. 32 *sub fin.* βούλομαι δὲ δὴ καὶ συλλογίσασθαι τὰ εἰρημένα κ.τ.λ.

[4] Cf. Kalinka, p. 52.

to the *De Comp. Verb.*, the conclusion is reached that the latter treatise intervened after c. 33, and that Dionysius extended the study of the style of Demosthenes to include his σύνθεσις, postponing consideration of the πραγματικὸς τόπος.

From the concluding paragraph of the *De Demosthene* it seems very probable that Dionysius sent the essay at once to Ammaeus without waiting to complete his study of the πραγματικὸς τόπος or to add his essays on Hyperides and Aeschines, for it is noticeable that Ammaeus is there addressed by name.[1] A copy of the complete essay on Demosthenes (which Dionysius now presumably circulated) found its way into the hands of Cn. Pompeius Geminus, whose objections to its remarks on Plato have already been mentioned.[2] It is probable therefore that the *Epistula ad Pompeium* is closely bound up in time with the *De Demosthene*, a considerable passage of which it quotes; and it seems not unlikely that the epistle immediately followed the essay on the style of Demosthenes.[3]

We may now turn to consider the position in the extant works of another letter which is also concerned with Demosthenes, though from quite a different point of view, the *Epistula ad Ammaeum* I. This letter was written in refutation of the statement of a contemporary philosopher, communicated by Ammaeus, to the effect that Demosthenes, in composing his speeches, closely followed the precepts of Aristotle's *Rhetoric*; and Dionysius, in rejecting the claim on chronological grounds, remarks that Demosthenes was indebted to quite different teachers, and promises a discussion of this subject with the words ὑπὲρ ὧν ἐν ἰδίᾳ δηλώσω γραφῇ τὰ δοκοῦντά μοι· πολὺς γὰρ ὁ περὶ αὐτῶν (*sc.* τῶν εἰσαγωγῶν) λόγος, ὃν οὐ καλῶς

---

[1] c. 58 (= I, 252) ταῦτα, ὦ κράτιστε ᾿Αμμαῖε, γράφειν εἴχομέν σοι περὶ τῆς Δημοσθένους λέξεως.

[2] Cf. above, p. 4.

[3] Kalinka, pp. 54–6, places the composition of *Ep. ad Pomp.* in the break after c. 33 (or c. 32, in his view) of the *De Dem.*, on the ground that Dionysius' censure of Plato in the first half of *De Dem.* is modified in *Ep. ad Pomp.* and turns to praise in *De Comp. Verb.* c. 19 and *De Dem.* c. 41. But (i) he has, as a result, to assume that the *De Dem.* was *published* after c. 32 was written, and there is no evidence at all for such an assumption; (ii) Dionysius' praise of Plato in *De Comp. Verb.* and *De Dem.* c. 41 is for his σύνθεσις—quite a different thing from the subject of his censure in the first half of *De Dem.*

εἶχεν ἑτέρας γραφῆς ποιῆσαι πάρεργον.¹ This has sometimes been thought to be a reference forward to our *De Demosthene*, but in that essay Dionysius' main concern is to prove the superiority of Demosthenes to his predecessors; any remarks which imply indebtedness of Demosthenes to them are merely introduced παρέργως, and do not represent the real subject of the essay, which is clearly outlined at the beginning of c. 33. The ἰδία γραφή promised, therefore, has either been lost, or was never composed. As this, the only piece of evidence which might have led to a more certain knowledge of the position in the series of *Ep. ad Ammaeum* I, fails us, it becomes necessary to resort to consideration of the letter itself. In it Dionysius not only contradicts the statement that the influence of Aristotle on Demosthenes was paramount, but also singles out for special mention Isaeus and Isocrates, as two rhetoricians whose precepts Demosthenes really did follow.² It is interesting to see the influence of Isaeus so clearly remarked; for this exactly corresponds with the statements of Dionysius in his *De Isaeo*, where Isaeus is πηγή τις . . . τῆς Δημοσθένους δυνάμεως.³ It seems therefore possible to argue that the theory of the contemporary Peripatetic philosopher was an attempt to outbid the *De Isaeo* and to give the credit for having influenced Demosthenes to Aristotle instead of to Isaeus; in other words, that the *Epistula ad Ammaeum* I is not (as has been commonly supposed, because of its lack of references to other previous essays) the earliest extant work of Dionysius, but was quite probably composed after the *De Lysia*, *De Isocrate*, and *De Isaeo* had been put into circulation and before the essay on the style of Demosthenes was commenced.⁴ Such an argument is, of course, far from clinching the matter; but where decisive evidence fails, hypothesis must take its place.

¹ *Ep. ad Amm.* I, c. 3 (= I, 259).
² c. 2 (= I, 258) ἵνα μὴ τοῦθ' ὑπολάβωσιν, ὅτι...οὐδ' ⟨ἂν⟩ αὐτὸς ὁ Δημοσθένης...τοσοῦτος ἐγένετο τοῖς 'Ισοκράτους τε καὶ 'Ισαίου κοσμούμενος παραγγέλμασιν, εἰ μὴ τὰς 'Αριστοτέλους τέχνας ἐξέμαθεν.
³ c. 3 (I, 95); cf. c. 7 (I, 101), c. 13 (I, 109), c. 20 (I, 123-4).
⁴ Kalinka's argument (pp. 57 ff.) that *Ep. ad Ammaeum* I was written after c. 8 of the *De Demosthene* (in which Kalinka mistakenly supposes Dionysius to underrate Isaeus' influence), and before c. 9, is perverse. There is no sign whatsoever of a break after c. 8, and the ἐγὼ μέν clause of c. 8 *sub fin.* is quite naturally and smoothly picked up by εἰ δὲ τὰ προσήκοντα ἔγνωκα in c. 9 *init.*

With the much more important essay on Thucydides we are fortunately on firmer ground; for in the opening passage of the second letter to Ammaeus, Dionysius says quite distinctly that he has already dealt with Thucydides, first in the essays on the orators dedicated to Ammaeus, and, "a little while ago", in the special essay on Thucydides.[1] His antithesis πρότερον μὲν ... ὀλίγοις δὲ δὴ πρόσθεν χρόνοις is clearly intended to mark the relative periods of composition of the essays on the orators and that on Thucydides. In the opening chapter of the *De Thucydide*, Dionysius gives further information; he has, he says, undertaken the work at the special request of Tubero, having postponed a treatise (πραγματεία) on Demosthenes (already commenced) in order to do so.[2] If it were possible to identify the work to which Dionysius alludes, there would be some evidence for deciding the amount of time which elapsed between the publication of the *De Demosthene* and that of the *De Thucydide*. That the reference can hardly be to the *De Demosthene* itself is suggested by Dionysius' use of the word πραγματεία: for the *De Demosthene* is, as has been already shown,[3] part of the series of essays on the orators, and is therefore only part of a σύνταξις, not a πραγματεία.[4] Nor is the view[5] that the reference is to the essay on the πραγματικὴ δεινότης of Demosthenes, promised at the end of the *De Demosthene*, satisfactory, if the occurrence of the word πραγματεία is to be pressed. It is therefore probable that the reference is to a treatise on the genuine and spurious speeches of Demosthenes on which Dionysius was engaged when drawing to

[1] *Ep. ad Amm.* II, 1 (= 1, 421) ἐγὼ μὲν ὑπελάμβανον ἀρκούντως δεδηλω-κέναι τὸν Θουκυδίδου χαρακτῆρα... πρότερον μὲν ἐν τοῖς περὶ τῶν ἀρχαίων ῥητόρων πρὸς τὸ σὸν ὄνομα συνταχθεῖσιν ὑπομνηματισμοῖς, ὀλίγοις ⟨δὲ⟩ δὴ πρόσθεν χρόνοις ἐν τῇ περὶ αὐτοῦ τοῦ Θουκυδίδου κατασκευασθείσῃ γραφῇ. Roberts misleadingly renders πρόσθεν as "before" instead of "ago".

[2] *De Thuc.* c. 1 (= 1, 326) σοῦ δὲ βουληθέντος ἰδίαν συντάξασθαί με περὶ Θουκυδίδου γραφὴν ἅπαντα περιειληφυῖαν τὰ δεόμενα λόγων, ἀναβαλόμενος τὴν περὶ Δημοσθένους πραγματείαν, ἣν εἶχον ἐν χερσίν, ὑπεσχόμην τε ποιήσειν, ὡς προῃροῦ, καὶ τελέσας τὴν ὑπόσχεσιν ἀποδίδωμι.

[3] Cf. above, pp. 27 ff. Kalinka, however (p. 60), considers the reference to be to the *De Dem.*, which he does not believe to have been originally planned as part of the work on the orators.

[4] See Rabe, *op. cit.* pp. 149–50.

[5] Blass, p. 22; Radermacher, *PW.* v, 1, col. 965.

the conclusion of his study of the style of Demosthenes.[1] If this is so, then the *De Thucydide* is not separated by a very wide interval of time from the extant *De Demosthene*.[2]

As it is already clear that the second epistle to Ammaeus followed closely on the publication of the *De Thucydide*, there remain only two essays which require to be placed. These are the *De Imitatione*, and the *De Dinarcho*. Some information regarding the composition of the former work is given by Dionysius in his Epistle to Pompeius (c. 3 *init.*); replying to Pompeius' request for an account of Herodotus and Xenophon he says: πεποίηκα [καὶ] τοῦτο οἷς ⟨πρὸς⟩ Δημήτριον ὑπεμνημάτισμαι[3] περὶ μιμήσεως. τούτων ὁ μὲν πρῶτος αὐτὴν περιείληφε τὴν περὶ τῆς μιμήσεως ζήτησιν, ὁ δὲ δεύτερος περὶ τοῦ τίνας ἄνδρας μιμεῖσθαι δεῖ ποιητάς τε καὶ φιλοσόφους, ἱστοριογράφους ⟨τε⟩ καὶ ῥήτορας, ὁ δὲ τρίτος περὶ τοῦ πῶς δεῖ μιμεῖσθαι μέχρι τοῦδε[4] ἀτελής. From these words it is clear that Dionysius had completed the first two books of the work when he wrote to Pompeius. It is possible to assume[5] that he had them beside him, delaying their publication until the third book was complete. But it is also possible that books 1 and 2 had already been published—perhaps a considerable time before; for it is clear from the work on the orators that Dionysius was in the habit of publishing his work piecemeal, and the fact that Pompeius, a philosopher with an enthusiasm for

[1] *De Dem.* c. 57 *sub fin.* ἐν ἑτέρᾳ δηλοῦταί μοι πραγματείᾳ τὰ περὶ Δημοσθένη (here again δηλοῦται is a strict present and Radermacher, *PW.* v, 965 is mistaken in saying "diese war fertig, als D. περὶ τῆς Δημοσθένους λέξεως schrieb"); cf. *De Dinarcho*, c. 11 ὡς ἐν τοῖς περὶ Δημοσθένους δεδηλώκαμεν and c. 13 ὡς ἀκριβέστερον περὶ αὐτῶν ἐν τῇ ⟨περὶ⟩ Δημοσθένους γραφῇ δεδηλώκαμεν. Cf. Rabe, *loc. cit.* and Usener, *Praef.* xxxv. For probable fragments of this treatise, see 1, 290–6.

[2] Kalinka, pp. 65–7, again introduces unnecessary complications by conjecturing that *De Thuc.* was composed between cc. 50 and 51 of the *De Dem.* Having taken τὴν περὶ Δημοσθένους πραγματείαν in *De Thuc.* c. 1 to be our *De Dem.*, he is obliged to look for a break in *De Dem.* in which the *De Thuc.* could have been composed; but the mere similarity of expression concerning οἰκονομία in *De Thuc.* c. 34 and *De Dem.* c. 51 is no evidence at all for his assumption.

[3] εἰς Δημήτριον ὑπομνηματισμόν MSS.; *corr.* Usener.

[4] περὶ τούτου δέ, MSS.

[5] Cf. Blass, p. 20, Roessler, p. 13, Rabe, p. 151, Roberts, p. 6, Egger, pp. 31–2.

Plato, had not heard of them, can hardly be held to be of any account. An examination of the epitome of book 2 leads to a strong conviction that the work was at least written, if not published, before Dionysius tackled the work on the orators. In his list of orators in the *De Imitatione* Dionysius names Lysias, Isocrates, Lycurgus, Demosthenes, Aeschines, and Hyperides, as worthy of imitation—thereby giving exactly the names mentioned in the Preface to the work on the orators with the one important difference that Lycurgus is introduced instead of Isaeus. It is extremely unlikely that after devoting a special essay to Isaeus, and pointing out his importance as a forerunner of Demosthenes, Dionysius would have omitted his name in a list of orators especially designed for imitation in the rhetorical schools.[1] There is therefore here a strong reason for believing that the *De Imitatione* (books 1 and 2) preceded the essays on the orators. Moreover, the criticism of Demosthenes in the *De Imitatione* quite fails to differentiate him from the other five orators as a model; it is hard to believe that Dionysius would have classed him thus *after* the praise he had lavished on him in the *De Demosthene*.[2] Books 1 and 2, therefore, of the *De Imitatione* were in all probability the earliest of Dionysius' critical works. Whether Book III was ever completed it is not possible to say; but to judge from the fact that no fragment of it is anywhere preserved, whereas several fragments belonging to Book 1 have been collected, it seems likely that this book too was one of the many studies which Dionysius never found time to complete.[3]

The remaining essay, the *De Dinarcho*, was certainly later than the work on the orators, as is apparent from its opening words.[4] It was also probably later than the *De Thucydide*, for the special treatise on Demosthenes mentioned in cc. 11 and 13 as already com-

[1] Cf. Kalinka, pp. 57 and 67-8. Weismann, p. 20, had placed the *De Imitatione* first, and the position is acknowledged as a possible one by Blass, p. 20.

[2] Cf. Ammon, *op. cit.* p. 98, n. 3 "tenuia quoque sunt, quae vet. cens. p. 433 R sq. de Demosthene traduntur, ut etiam in Libro II περὶ μιμήσεως Dionysius imaginem summi oratoris parum distincte expressisse videatur."

[3] The opening words of the *De Thucydide* (ἐν τοῖς προεκδοθεῖσι περὶ τῆς μιμήσεως ὑπομνηματισμοῖς κ.τ.λ.) do not prove that Book III had been added.

[4] Cf. above, p. 30.

pleted (ὡς . . . δεδηλώκαμεν) is in all probability that which Dionysius was engaged in composing when he was concluding the *De Demosthene* and which he temporarily abandoned in order to write the *De Thucydide* for Tubero. Moreover, the *De Dinarcho* is the only extant essay of Dionysius which is not addressed to any friend; it reads more like a rapidly compiled series of notes than a finished literary product, and it may well be regarded, therefore, as the last of the extant literary works. In the present study, however, its position in the series will not be of great account, for it is not primarily a work of literary criticism in the true sense; its professed object is, not to give an impartial account of the merits and faults of Dinarchus, but to offer a list of his genuine works and those which are to be condemned as spurious.[1] Such criticism as there is in the essay is subordinate to this main purpose, and it will therefore be treated as standing apart from the main study, which is to be concerned with the essays of primarily critical interest.

According to this examination, the order of composition of the extant essays was as follows:

(1) *De Imitatione*, Books 1 and 2.
(2) *De Lysia, De Isocrate, De Isaeo.*
(3) *Ep. ad Ammaeum* I.
(4) *De Demosthene* cc. 1–33.
(5) *De Compositione Verborum.*
(6) *De Demosthene* cc. 34–end.
(7) *Ep. ad Pompeium.*
(8) *De Thucydide.*
(9) *Ep. ad Ammaeum* II.
(10) *De Dinarcho.*

In brief, it may be said that the evidence inclines, but does not force us to place nos. 1, 3, 7 and 10 in their present positions, but that the remaining essays, which represent the bulk of Dionysius' critical work, could hardly have been produced in any other order. With this assurance, therefore, we may proceed to consider the critic's outlook and, in particular, his method in each essay in turn, and to undertake the hitherto unattempted task of deciding whether there may be said to be any development in his powers of critical exposition.

---

[1] Cf. c. 1 (= 1, 297) διορίσαι τούς τε γνησίους καὶ ψευδεῖς λόγους κ.τ.λ. and c. 4 *init.*

CHAPTER III

The earlier essays—on imitation, on Lysias, on Isocrates, and on Isaeus

ALTHOUGH the essay on Imitation does not survive in its original form, the epitome of the second book together with the excerpt in *Epistula ad Pompeium* enables us to form an opinion of its merits and defects as a work of criticism. The epitome itself does not represent a very drastic reduction of Dionysius' original remarks, as may be seen from a comparison of the sections on the historians (c. 3, ii, 207–210) with the full treatment of them in the excerpt quoted in the letter to Pompeius (c. 3, ii, 232–248). The epitomator very briefly dismisses the lengthy study of the πραγματικὸς τόπος of Herodotus and Thucydides given in his original; but it is noticeable that he adheres very closely to the text of Dionysius in his summary of the λεκτικὸς τόπος. It is possible therefore to accept the epitome as representing the gist of Dionysius' remarks on the style of the authors mentioned in it.

The essay on Imitation is, as its title immediately suggests, a purely practical handbook for use in the rhetorical schools. Its close affinities with the tenth book of Quintilian (i, §§ 46–84) have long since been observed;[1] and although it is still not quite certain how far Quintilian was indebted to Dionysius,[2] and how far they both used a common source,[3] it is at any rate clear that they both entered upon literary criticism with a strong rhetorical bias. So Dionysius

---

[1] H. Stephanus, who was the first to publish the epitome (Paris, 1554), is followed by Sylburg, Hudson, Holwell, and Reiske in his comparisons of Dionysius with Quintilian.

[2] The early editors, followed by (*inter alios*) Claussen, *Quaestiones Quintilianeae* (Fleckeisen's Jahrbücher, Suppl. VI) and W. Heydenreich, *De Quintiliani inst. or. libro* X, *de D. H. de imitatione libro* II, *de canone, qui dicitur, Alexandrino* (Erlangen, 1900), uphold this view.

[3] As is the opinion of Usener, *Dionysii Halicarnassensis Librorum de Imitatione Reliquiae etc.* (Bonn, 1889), pp. 110 ff.; cf. Nettleship, *Lectures and Essays, Second Series* (Oxford, 1895), p. 83.

constantly stresses those characteristics of the authors under consideration which are likely to prove of service to his pupils; the great writers of Greek poetry and prose are throughout criticised for their rhetorical, not their inherent value. It is observed that the poems of Alcaeus, if the metre be removed, frequently provide political harangues;[1] Euripides is recognised to be fully conversant with rhetorical doctrine;[2] Philistus is more valuable than Thucydides as a model for forensic oratory;[3] Homer is to be imitated for his power of arousing the emotions and of delineating character;[4] the emotional effect of the poems of Simonides is duly noted for imitation.[5] In fact, in no less than seven out of eleven criticisms of the poets is stress laid on their ἤθη or ἤθη καὶ πάθη.[6] Whatever the literary genre, be it epic, tragedy, or lyric, be it history or philosophy, the rhetorician makes no distinction; all writers for him form a single quarry from which he may draw material for the all-important study of effective public speaking.

But not only is the general aim and outlook of the critic rhetorical; his methods of criticism are also dominated by the rhetorical system. In the excerpt on the historians quoted in the letter to Pompeius, Herodotus and Thucydides, Xenophon, Philistus, and Theopompus are each criticised first according to their merits and defects in the realm of subject-matter (πραγματικὸς τόπος), and secondly according to their characteristics in style (λεκτικὸς τόπος). The former heading is in each instance subdivided, and five duties (ἔργα) of the historian in the sphere of subject-matter provide the basis of the criticism throughout. The historian must, first of all, select an attractive subject which will appeal to his readers; secondly, he must know where to begin and where to end; thirdly, he must know what to

---

[1] II, 205 πολλαχοῦ γοῦν τὸ μέτρον τις εἰ περιέλοι, ῥητορείαν ἂν εὕροι πολιτικήν.

[2] II, 206 ὁ δὲ Εὐριπίδης πολὺς ἐν ταῖς ῥητορικαῖς εἰσαγωγαῖς.

[3] II, 209 (cf. 244) Θουκυδίδου ⟨δὲ⟩ πρὸς τοὺς ἀληθεῖς ἀγῶνας ὠφελιμώτερος.

[4] II, 204 λάβε ζῆλον ἠθῶν τε τῶν ἐκεῖ καὶ παθῶν.

[5] II, 205 τὸ οἰκτίζεσθαι μὴ μεγαλοπρεπῶς ἀλλὰ παθητικῶς.

[6] Viz. Homer, Pindar, Simonides, Stesichorus, Alcaeus, Aeschylus, and Sophocles; Euripides is tested but found wanting; the writers of comedy are also ἠθικοί.

include and what to leave out; fourthly, he must be careful to arrange his narrative in the correct order; and lastly (Dionysius adds this almost as an afterthought!) he must be impartial. Herodotus and Thucydides are considered at length (II, 232–238) according to these five divisions (Thucydides being manifestly unfairly treated and favour being shown by the critic to his fellow countryman); and their presence is equally noticeable in the criticisms of Xenophon (II, 241), Philistus (II, 242–3), and Theopompus (II, 244). The λεκτικὸς τόπος is also subdivided; occasionally criticisms appear on the basis of an author's ἐκλογή as opposed to his σύνθεσις,[1] but most characteristic in this branch of study is the use of the virtues of style, which are noticeable throughout the treatise,[2] and particularly in the treatment of the λεκτικὸς τόπος of the historians. The essay is, in fact, a perfect example of the defects of the method of criticism by "literary labels",[3] when it is used by a critic who fails to make personal contact with his author, and who is lacking in the one quality which might redeem his work, that is, epigrammatic power.

The mechanical method of criticism by ἀρεταὶ λέξεως nowhere finds a better illustration than in the criticism of the style of Herodotus and Thucydides, which Dionysius himself quotes in the letter to Pompeius (II, 239–40). The system of virtues is clearly set forth, and the styles of the two historians are tested for each virtue in turn. In fact the critical study of Herodotus and Thucydides amounts to little more than a series of notes informing the reader that they do or do not possess each particular virtue. The result may accordingly be tabulated as follows:

Virtue	Verdict
1. Purity of language	Both are accurate in this respect
2. Lucidity	Herodotus indisputably superior
3. Brevity	Thucydides is superior
4. Vividness	Both are sufficiently successful to be imitated

[1] E.g. II, 205 Σιμωνίδου δὲ παρατήρει τὴν ἐκλογὴν τῶν ὀνομάτων, τῆς συνθέσεως τὴν ἀκρίβειαν, II, 242 ἐκλέγει δὲ... καὶ συντίθησιν. . . .

[2] Cf. especially the criticisms of Pindar and Alcaeus.

[3] Other interesting examples, apart from Quintilian, of this type of criticism are Cicero, De Orat. III, 28, Hortensius frag. XVII and XVIII (Usener); Horace, Epp. II, 1, 55 ff.; cf. D'Alton, op. cit., p. 542.

5. Character-drawing and   The honours are divided; Thucydides
   emotional power   for emotional power, Herodotus for
                               character-drawing
6. Magnificence   The two are equal
7. Vigour and power   Thucydides is superior
8. Charm and persuasiveness Herodotus far superior
9. Propriety   Herodotus is rather better

It clearly did not require a great deal of thought or originality to produce a work such as this; for the critic's only function is to apply to the authors whom he criticises a code which has already been formulated for him. It is true that the form of Dionysius' work precluded him from illustrating or defending his remarks;[1] but he shows no sign of discrimination, of insight, of personal taste or enthusiasm; he is merely a calculator, a mechanical worker dogmatically stating his results for undisputed acceptance by his pupils. His essay is full of comparative criticism, yet there is little that can be considered enlightening; the smoothness of Hesiod is contrasted with the roughness of Antimachus,[2] the sublimity of Aeschylus and the dignity of Sophocles with the everyday tones of Euripides;[3] Xenophon is compared with Herodotus,[4] Philistus with Thucydides;[5] yet the reader each time comes away with the feeling that Dionysius is as yet rather a superficial critic, a master, no doubt, of the intricacies of rhetoric, but the merest tiro in an art which calls for sympathy and power of personal expression rather than the ability to amass knowledge and marshal facts.

[1] *De Thuc.* c. 1 (= 1, 325) συντόμῳ τε καὶ κεφαλαιώδει γραφῇ περιλαβών, οὐ δι᾽ ὀλιγωρίαν καὶ ῥᾳστώνην οὐδὲ διὰ σπάνιν τῶν δυνησομένων βεβαιῶσαι τὰς προθέσεις, ἀλλὰ τῆς εὐκαιρίας τῶν γραφομένων στοχαζόμενος, ὡς καὶ περὶ τῶν ἄλλων ἐποίησα. οὐ γὰρ ἦν ἀκριβῆ καὶ διεξοδικὴν δήλωσιν ὑπὲρ ἑκάστου τῶν ἀνδρῶν ποιεῖσθαι, προελόμενον εἰς ἐλάχιστον ὄγκον συναγαγεῖν τὴν πραγματείαν.

[2] II, 204 Ἡσίοδος μὲν γὰρ ἐφρόντισεν ἡδονῆς δι᾽ ὀνομάτων λειότητος καὶ συνθέσεως ἐμμελοῦς. ᾿Αντίμαχος δὲ εὐτονίας καὶ ἀγωνιστικῆς τραχύτητος καὶ τοῦ συνήθους τῆς ἐξαλλαγῆς.

[3] II, 206 ὁ δ᾽ οὖν Αἰσχύλος πρῶτος ὑψηλός τε καὶ τῆς μεγαλοπρεπείας ἐχόμενος...Σοφοκλῆς δὲ ἔν τε τοῖς ⟨ἤθεσι καὶ τοῖς⟩ πάθεσι διήνεγκεν τὸ τῶν προσώπων ἀξίωμα τηρῶν. Εὐριπίδη μέντοι τὸ ὅλον ἀληθὲς καὶ προσεχὲς τῷ βίῳ τῷ νῦν ἤρεσεν.

[4] II, 208 ὁ μὲν Ξενοφῶν Ἡροδότου ζηλωτὴς ἐγένετο κ.τ.λ.

[5] *Ib.* Φίλιστος δὲ μιμητής ἐστι Θουκυδίδου κ.τ.λ.

However, when Dionysius, after publishing, or at any rate composing, the first two books of the *De Imitatione*, turned to write his essays on the orators, he proceeded to a series of studies which gave him full scope for the exercise of any critical powers he possessed. It becomes interesting, therefore, to see how Dionysius used his opportunity, and whether any improvement in outlook or method is to be observed.

The *De Lysia*, which it is necessary to examine first, reveals an outlook hardly less rhetorical than the *De Imitatione*, for the whole essay is dedicated to the purpose of μίμησις. In many respects Lysias is recommended as a model, and most of his virtues are "worthy of imitation and emulation".[1] Where Lysias is successful Dionysius bids his pupils (κελεύω is his word)[2] take over the virtues; where he is unsuccessful other and better models must be sought. A naïve touch, significant as anything in the essay of the rhetorical attitude to style, is to be found in the chapter on brevity (c. 5 = 1, 13); there Dionysius informs his readers that Lysias' brevity renders his style an excellent model for an ordinary individual who desires merely to state his case, but is far from being sufficient for a rhetorician, who desires to make a display of his powers—ὡς μὲν ἰδιώτῃ δηλῶσαι βουλομένῳ τὰ πράγματα ἀποχρῶν, ὡς δὲ ῥήτορι περιουσίαν δυνάμεως ἐνδείξασθαι ζητοῦντι οὐχ ἱκανός.

If we next turn to the methods of criticism employed in the *De Lysia*, we find that the virtues of style, though they are not set forth quite so undisguisedly as in the *De Imitatione*, still form a very obvious framework, at any rate in the first ten chapters. After a brief and very insufficient[3] account of the orator's life, his style is subjected to a number of tests. In the first place, his language is said to be a living model of Attic Greek as it was spoken in his day; purity is in fact one of the strongest characteristics in his style.[4] Accuracy, too, which results from the use of ordinary current words, is found to be a second characteristic.[5] The lucidity of Lysias is such that he appeals quite as much to the amateur as to the professional

---

[1] 1, 9, 12, 13, 17, 26, 30, etc.   [2] c. 3 (= 1, 12).
[3] Cf. Egger, *op. cit.* p. 47.
[4] c. 2 (= 1, 9), καθαρός ἐστι τὴν ἑρμηνείαν πάνυ καὶ τῆς Ἀττικῆς γλώττης ἄριστος κανών.
[5] c. 3 (= 1, 10).

44 DIONYSIUS OF HALICARNASSUS

speaker.¹ He has moreover accomplished the difficult feat of combining brevity with lucidity; the secret of his success being his refusal to allow the matter to be slave to the manner.² Yet the lucidity and brevity of Lysias do not result in bareness; his style is not merely that of the expositor, for he polishes his expressions and brings them out in full and rounded fashion.³ He possesses, moreover, vividness, power of character-representation, and propriety. His vividness, "the power of representing the action as though it were taking place beneath the listeners' gaze", is so remarkable that any but the stupid or overcritical can feel that they are witnessing the action and even conversing with the characters.⁴ His character-drawing manifests itself in three branches, the thoughts, the diction, and the composition of his speakers. "Lysias makes his characters think honourable, just, and moderate thoughts, so that their speeches seem to be models of conduct."⁵ Their vocabulary, too, is that of the everyday world around them, for Lysias realized that "pomposity, strange words, and the appearance of deliberateness all spoil character-drawing".⁶ Finally, the composition of the speakers in Lysias is remarkably simple and artless; but "this very appearance of naturalness is artificial, the loosely-strung sentence is bound up, and beneath the very semblance of artlessness the art is concealed".⁷ Propriety, too, is everywhere observed; Lysias takes care to differentiate between young and old, high-born and humble, and pays attention to the nature of the audience and the occasion.⁸ Persuasiveness and charm abound in his work.⁹ However, Lysias has his failings, and is by no means a perfect model. "Lysias' style is not lofty and magnificent, and most decidedly not striking and impressive; it does not reveal pungency, power, or severity, and

¹ c. 4 (= I, 12) ἡ δὲ Λυσίου λέξις ἅπασά ἐστι φανερὰ καὶ σαφὴς καὶ τῷ πάνυ πόρρω δοκοῦντι πολιτικῶν ἀφεστάναι λόγων.
² Ib. καὶ μὴν τό γε βραχέως ἐκφέρειν τὰ νοήματα μετὰ τοῦ σαφῶς, χαλεποῦ πράγματος ὄντος κ.τ.λ. . . . οὐ τοῖς ὀνόμασι δουλεύει τὰ πράγματα κ.τ.λ.
³ c. 6 (= I, 14) ἡ συστρέφουσα τὰ νοήματα καὶ στρογγύλως ἐκφέρουσα λέξις.
⁴ c. 7 (= I, 14–15). ⁵ c. 8 (= I, 15).
⁶ Ib. ὁ γὰρ ὄγκος καὶ τὸ ξένον καὶ τὸ ἐξ ἐπιτηδεύσεως ἅπαν ἀνηθοποίητον.
⁷ Ib. (= I, 16) πεποίηται γὰρ αὐτῷ τοῦτο τὸ ἀποίητον καὶ δέδεται τὸ λελυμένον καὶ ἐν αὐτῷ τῷ μὴ δοκεῖν δεινῶς κατεσκευάσθαι τὸ δεινὸν ἔχει.
⁸ c. 9 (= I, 16). ⁹ c. 10 init. (= I, 17).

possesses neither grip nor intensity. It is not full of passion and spirit, and though it convinces in its portrayal of character, it does not impress in its appeals to the emotions. It cannot enforce the attention in the same way that it can delight, persuade, and charm. In short, it is sure rather than venturesome, and not capable of revealing the power of art so much as of resembling the truth of nature."[1]

It is clear that the system of virtues given in the *De Imitatione* is here applied to the criticism of Lysias; for purity (c. 2), accuracy (c. 3), lucidity (c. 4), brevity (c. 5), compactness (c. 6), vividness (c. 7), character-portrayal (c. 8), appropriateness (c. 9) and persuasiveness (c. 10) are the pegs on which the remarks of Dionysius are hung. The list given in the *De Imitatione* is followed with remarkable closeness; there is a slight elaboration, since accuracy is ranked as a separate virtue,[2] and compactness (τὸ στρογγύλον) is for the first time introduced; but apart from these the ἀρεταί stand in almost exactly the same order as they do in the earlier work. A further interesting revelation of the mechanical method pursued is to be found later in the essay (c. 24 *init.* = 1, 34), where Dionysius praises a proem of Lysias because ἁπάσας ἔχει τὰς ἀρετάς, ὅσας δεῖ τὸ προοίμιον ἔχειν and adds δηλώσουσι δὲ οἱ κανόνες αὐτῷ παρατεθέντες οἱ τῶν τεχνῶν (cf. below ταῦτα μὲν δὴ παραγγέλλουσι ποιεῖν οἱ τεχνογράφοι and ὧδέ πως τεχνολογοῦσιν). He does not at this point appear to have observed that he was merely arguing in a circle, for the τεχνογράφοι must have utilised Lysias himself in forming the very list of virtues which he was now, in all naïveté, "discovering" in Lysias.[3] Curiously enough, a few chapters before (c. 18), Dionysius had admitted that the rules given in the τέχναι for the narrative part of a speech were largely drawn from a study of Lysias himself.[4] It must, however, be said that although the stylistic

---

[1] c. 13 (= 1, 23).

[2] I do not agree with C. N. Smiley, *C.P.* 1 (1906), p. 413, that in the excerpt from *De Imit.* in *Ep. ad Pomp.* (c. 3 = 11, 239) ἀκρίβεια is to be regarded as a separate virtue (represented by the word ἀκριβοῦσιν); his argument quite fails to account for the lack of any specific mention of σαφήνεια, which has rightly led editors to assume a lacuna.

[3] Cf. D'Alton, *op. cit.* p. 560.

[4] 1, 29 οἴομαι δὲ καὶ τὰς τέχνας τῶν λόγων, ἐν αἷς εἴρηταί ⟨τι⟩ περὶ διηγήσεως ἀξιόλογον, οὐκ ἐξ ἄλλων τινῶν μᾶλλον ἢ τῶν ὑπὸ Λυσίου γραφεισῶν εἰληφέναι τὰ παραγγέλματα καὶ τὰς ἀφορμάς.

system as it stood at this point of its evolution clearly forms the foundation of the essay on Lysias, there is much in the super-structure that is, or appears to be, original, is worth saying, and well said.

The use of the code of virtues is not by any means the only indication of rhetorical doctrine in the *De Lysia*; the essay is remarkable for the number of technical divisions, so dear to the heart of the rhetorician, to be found in it. Not content with using a list of virtues which had already gone a very long way from Aristotle and Theophrastus, Dionysius proceeds to split the individual virtues. His introduction of ἀκρίβεια as a separate virtue has already been noticed; a similar instance of this tendency to divide is seen in his remarks on σαφήνεια (c. 4), which is to be considered as manifesting itself not only in the style of an author (λεκτικὴ σαφήνεια) but in his treatment of subject-matter (πραγματικὴ σαφήνεια). The virtue of ἠθοποιΐα, or character-portrayal, is likewise subjected to a threefold division, and is said to manifest itself in the thoughts, the diction, and the composition of the speaker.[1] The virtue of propriety is similarly divided, and is treated as appearing in relation to the speaker, the audience, and the subject.[2] So in dealing with the πραγματικὸς χαρακτήρ of Lysias, Dionysius considers the subject from the aspects of inventive power (εὕρεσις), selection of arguments (κρίσις), and arrangement (τάξις or οἰκονομία);[3] and in selecting his examples of Lysias' style, he follows the old tradition which divided oratory into forensic, deliberative, and epideictic.[4] Finally, his examination of the powers of Lysias in the various parts of a speech is based upon the well-known tradition, ascribed by Dionysius to

---

[1] c. 8 (= I, 15) τριῶν τε ὄντων, ἐν οἷς καὶ περὶ ἃ τὴν ἀρετὴν εἶναι ταύτην συμβέβηκε, διανοίας τε καὶ λέξεως καὶ τρίτης τῆς συνθέσεως κ.τ.λ. Cf. Demetrius Π. Ἑρμ. § 38 for a similar division of τὸ μεγαλοπρεπές.

[2] c. 9 (= I, 16) πρός τε τὸν λέγοντα καὶ πρὸς τοὺς ἀκούοντας καὶ πρὸς τὸ πρᾶγμα. Cf. Cicero, *Orator*, §§ 70-1.

[3] c. 15 (= I, 25) εὑρετικὸς γάρ ἐστι...κριτικὸς ὢν δεῖ λέγειν...τάξει δὲ ἁπλῇ τινι κέχρηται, κ.τ.λ.

[4] c. 16 (= I, 26) τριχῇ δὲ νενεμημένου τοῦ ῥητορικοῦ λόγου καὶ τρία περιειληφότος διάφορα τοῖς τέλεσι γένη, τό τε δικανικὸν καὶ τὸ συμβουλευτικὸν καὶ τὸ καλούμενον ἐπιδεικτικὸν ἢ πανηγυρικόν, κ.τ.λ. Yet another threefold division appears in c. 19 (= I, 31).

THE EARLIER ESSAYS 47

Isocrates and his followers, which rigidly divided every speech into proem, narrative, proofs, and epilogue.[1]

From the point of view, therefore, of general outlook and critical method, the *De Lysia* cannot be said to be much in advance of the *De Imitatione*. It is noticeable that there is as yet no illustration of criticisms made; for the passages of Lysias appended to the study are merely set παραδείγματα intended to give a general idea of his manner in each of the three branches of oratory.[2] Though excellently chosen, they may well have been part of the rhetorician's stock-in-trade. Nowhere does Dionysius adduce any evidence to prove that Lysias possesses the qualities attributed to him, and nowhere is a single sentence of Lysias subjected to any kind of critical analysis. Many of Dionysius' statements have to be accepted without question, and although there is undoubtedly a very great deal of truth in what he says, his powers of critical exposition remain as yet undeveloped.

There is, however, one important respect in which the *De Lysia* is greatly superior to the *De Imitatione*: in his study of Lysias, Dionysius has undoubtedly made personal contact with his author. Superficiality was, we found, one of the chief faults of the *De Imitatione*; in the *De Lysia* Dionysius fully expresses his appreciation of the individuality of Lysias. The tenth and eleventh chapters of the essay afford the best evidence of this, for there Dionysius, having drawn, perhaps somewhat impatiently, to the end of his list of virtues, having applied his code, approved and disapproved, still feels that he has failed to express the most characteristic trait of all— the inexplicable charm which marks all Lysias' work.[3] In his endeavour to express the nature and effect of this quality, his mind wanders to kindred spheres; the χάρις of Lysias is like the harmony of music or the grace of the human form. Then he admits that this quality is not to be expressed by rational argument, but must

---

[1] c. 16 (= I, 27) διαιρήσομαι δὲ αὐτάς, ὡς Ἰσοκράτει τε καὶ τοῖς κατ' ἐκεῖνον τὸν ἄνδρα κοσμουμένοις ἤρεσεν.

[2] cc. 23, 25, 27 (from the Κατὰ Διογείτονος, forensic); c. 30 (from the Ὀλυμπικός, epideictic); c. 33 (from the Περὶ τοῦ μὴ καταλῦσαι τὴν πάτριον πολιτείαν, deliberative).

[3] c. 10 (= I, 18) ἡ πᾶσιν ἐπανθοῦσα τοῖς ὀνόμασι κἀπ' ἴσης χάρις, πρᾶγμα παντὸς κρεῖττον λόγου καὶ θαυμασιώτερον.

be recognised by instinctive feeling;[1] its presence, realised by the criterion of this ἄλογος αἴσθησις, is the surest ultimate guide when there is any doubt concerning the genuineness of a speech.[2] This passage, coming as it does directly after the formal, systematic criticism of the previous nine chapters, clearly marks a distinct advance, being in itself an admission of the ultimate insufficiency of mechanical criticism and an acknowledgement of the supreme importance of personal contact with the author whose work is being criticised.[3]

We may now proceed to examine the *De Isocrate*, which immediately follows the *De Lysia* in order of composition. This essay is constructed on the same plan as the *De Lysia*; a brief sketch of the orator's life (c. 1) is followed by consideration of his merits and defects in style (cc. 2–3) and subject-matter (cc. 4–10); a brief summary of the results obtained is added (cc. 11–12), the critic's agreement with earlier writers on certain deficiencies of Isocrates is recorded and explained (cc. 13–14), and the study concludes with a series of illustrative passages (cc. 15–20). Nor are these affinities to the *De Lysia* confined to form; the rhetorical outlook is again predominant, and stress is repeatedly laid on the principle of μίμησις. The subject-matter of Isocrates is highly commended on the ground that it is calculated to strengthen those virtues which are especially needed in the citizen, namely patriotism, courage, justice, orderliness, and obedience.[4] But the style of Isocrates, judged from the point of view of its value for purposes of declamation, is found wanting; for the artificiality of its composition and the monotony of its period-construction render it suitable only for a reader.[5] It is,

---

[1] c. 11 (= 1, 19) αἰσθήσει γὰρ τούτων ἕκαστον καταλαμβάνεται καὶ οὐ λόγῳ.

[2] *Ib.* καὶ ὅταν διαπορῶ περί τινος τῶν ἀναφερομένων εἰς αὐτὸν λόγων, καὶ μὴ ῥᾴδιον ᾖ μοι διὰ τῶν ἄλλων σημείων τἀληθὲς εὑρεῖν, ἐπὶ ταύτην καταφεύγω τὴν ἀρετὴν ὡς ἐπὶ ψῆφον ἐσχάτην.

[3] This is briefly acknowledged by Egger, *op. cit.* p. 50; cf. D'Alton, *op. cit.* p. 544.

[4] c. 4 (= 1, 60) κράτιστα γὰρ δὴ παιδεύματα πρὸς ἀρετὴν ἐν τοῖς Ἰσοκράτους ἔστιν εὑρεῖν λόγοις κ.τ.λ. and cc. 5–10 *passim*.

[5] c. 2 (= 1, 57) τῶν τε γὰρ φωνηέντων τὰς παραλλήλους θέσεις ὡς ἐκλυούσας τὰς ἁρμονίας τῶν ἤχων καὶ τὴν λειότητα τῶν φθόγγων λυμαινομένας περιΐσταται, περιόδῳ τε καὶ κύκλῳ περιλαμβάνειν τὰ νοήματα

moreover, lacking in that essential quality—the power to stir the emotions.[1] On the subject of Isocrates' artificiality and lack of emotional power, Dionysius makes many sound and interesting remarks; but we note the deepening of the rhetorical shadow in this essay, in which an author is condemned as unsuitable for a purpose which his work was never intended to serve.

However, not only the general outlook, but the method of criticism adopted, particularly in the earlier chapters, reveals the influence of rhetorical theory. The list of virtues clearly underlies the treatment of Isocrates' style in cc. 2–3. The orator's style is pure, no word being carelessly introduced (τὸ καθαρόν); it preserves the common idiom with the greatest accuracy (ἀκρίβεια), avoiding archaic, obscure, and affected expressions, and making only moderate use of figurative language. It is, moreover, lucid (σαφήνεια), but brevity (συντομία) and compactness (τὸ στρογγύλον) are not to be found in it. Vividness (ἐνάργεια), power of representing character (ἠθοποιΐα), persuasiveness (τὸ πιθανόν), and appropriateness (τὸ πρέπον) are also its characteristics. It lacks the power to stir (πάθος), and it has only a rather formal charm (χάρις), but it makes up for this in loftiness (ὕψος), magnificence (τὸ μεγαλοπρεπές), and dignity (ἀξίωμα).

Comparative criticism in the *De Isocrate* is also strongly influenced by the system of ἀρεταί.[2] The style of Isocrates is contrasted at most points with that of Lysias, and although Dionysius occasionally makes a happy remark, such as πέφυκε γὰρ ἡ Λυσίου λέξις ἔχειν τὸ χαρίεν, ἡ δὲ Ἰσοκράτους βούλεται,[3] which neatly sums up the position, he is still dominated in his comparisons by the list of virtues. His summary in the 11th chapter shows this clearly, and his treatment there of Lysias and Isocrates is strongly reminiscent of his treatment of Herodotus and Thucydides in the *De Imitatione*.[4]

πειρᾶται ῥυθμοειδεῖ πάνυ καὶ οὐ πολὺ ἀπέχοντι τοῦ ποιητικοῦ μέτρου, ἀναγνώσεώς τε μᾶλλον οἰκειότερός ἐστιν ἢ χρήσεως. Cf. the criticism of Hieronymus cited in c. 13 (= 1, 73).

[1] c. 2 (= 1, 57) τοιγάρτοι τὰς μὲν ἐπιδείξεις τὰς ἐν ταῖς πανηγύρεσι καὶ τὴν ἐκ χειρὸς θεωρίαν φέρουσιν αὐτοῦ οἱ λόγοι, τοὺς δὲ ἐν ἐκκλησίαις καὶ δικαστηρίοις ἀγῶνας οὐχ ὑπομένουσι. τούτου δὲ αἴτιον, ὅτι πολὺ τὸ παθητικὸν ἐν ἐκείνοις εἶναι δεῖ. Again cf. the criticism of Hieronymus in c. 13.

[2] c. 2 *init*. (= 1, 56).   [3] c. 3 (= 1, 59).   [4] Cf. p. 41 above.

In purity of language the two orators are equally good; in accurate use of current idiom they are also alike, except that Isocrates introduces a little more figurative expression; they are both masters of lucidity and vividness, but in brevity Lysias is the more successful; in amplification Isocrates wins, but in power of condensation Lysias; in character-representation both are skilful, but in charm Lysias is indisputably superior; Isocrates, however, has magnificence, while neither lacks persuasiveness and appropriateness; in composition Lysias is more simple, Isocrates more elaborate, and in short Lysias is more convincing in portraying the truth, and Isocrates is more powerful in grappling with a complicated structure. Here again what Dionysius says commands ready agreement, but the way in which he says it is stereotyped and involves little or no creative effort.

Further influence of the rhetorical system is to be seen in the subdivisions according to which style and subject-matter are considered. The style of Isocrates is discussed from the point of view of its vocabulary (ἐκλογή), its composition (σύνθεσις), and its figures (σχήματα), according to the three-fold division [1] mentioned above [2] which occurs in the *Auctor ad Herennium* [3] and is ascribed by Dionysius to Theophrastus. Similarly the treatment of subject-matter is divided into inventiveness (εὕρεσις), selection of arguments (κρίσις), arrangement of arguments (τάξις), and other technical headings; [4] it is true that they do not dominate Dionysius' discussion as does the stylistic system, but they afford further evidence of the rhetorical approach.

However, the improvement noted already in the *De Lysia* in the making of personal contact with the author criticised is here maintained; for the chapters in which Dionysius paraphrases the arguments of portions of the *Panegyricus* (c. 5), the *Philippus* (c. 6), the *De Pace* (c. 7), the *Areopagiticus* (c. 8), and the *Archidamus* (c. 9) reveal a strong appreciation of the nobility of Isocrates' ideas, and a real enthusiasm for his work. In each of these chapters, with their

---

[1] c. 3 *init.* (= 1, 58) καθόλου δὲ τριῶν ὄντων, ὡς φησι Θεόφραστος, ἐξ ὧν γίνεται τὸ μέγα καὶ σεμνὸν καὶ περιττὸν ἐν λέξει, τῆς τε ἐκλογῆς τῶν ὀνομάτων, καὶ τῆς ἐκ τούτων ἁρμονίας καὶ τῶν περιλαμβανόντων αὐτὰ σχημάτων, ἐκλέγει μὲν...ἁρμόττει δὲ...σχηματίζει δὲ κ.τ.λ.

[2] See p. 21.

[3] IV, 12, 17 (Demetrius Π. Ἑρμ. § 38 substitutes διάνοια for σχήματα).

[4] c. 4 *init.* (= 1, 60).

vigorous, opening rhetorical questions, Dionysius has freed himself for the moment of technical *minutiae* and caught something of the spirit of Isocrates at his best.

There is, finally, one respect in which Dionysius has made a great advance on his previous essays, that is in his introduction for the first time of detailed analysis of the author criticised. In the *De Lysia* he had merely given stock παραδείγματα of his author's style, without any kind of comment. In the *De Isocrate* he gives similar παραδείγματα of a deliberative and a forensic oration of Isocrates (cc. 16, 17, 19). But in c. 14 of the essay he goes farther than this; he is not satisfied with a mere statement of the merits and faults of Isocrates' style, and a selection of passages which the reader has to examine and appraise for himself; instead, he sets out to prove that he is justified in condemning Isocrates for excessive use of antithesis, parisosis, paromoiosis and the like, by quoting and examining no less than eight short passages from the *Panegyricus* (§§ 75 ff.).[1] Some of these may be summarised, as examples of a very important development here noticeable for the first time. On the sentence πλείστων μὲν οὖν ἀγαθῶν αἰτίους καὶ μεγίστων ἐπαίνων ἀξίους ἡγοῦμαι Dionysius comments "here not only is phrase parallel to phrase, but word is parallel to word, for πλείστων is balanced by μεγίστων, ἀγαθῶν by ἐπαίνων, and αἰτίους by ἀξίους". Similarly in the sentence οὐδὲ ἀπέλαυον μὲν ὡς ἰδίων, ἠμέλουν δὲ ὡς ἀλλοτρίων, ἀλλὰ ἐκήδοντο μὲν ὡς οἰκείων, ἀπείχοντο δὲ ὥσπερ χρὴ τῶν μηδὲν προσηκόντων he remarks on the recurring antitheses, ἀπέλαυον contrasted with ἠμέλουν, ἰδίων with ἀλλοτρίων, ἐκήδοντο with ἀπείχοντο, and οἰκείων with μηδὲν προσηκόντων. Nor is Dionysius pedantic in his objections; he is perfectly agreeable to an occasional parallelism or antithesis; but he does object vigorously to an un-limited number of them. His point of view, and his insistence on the principle of the mean,[2] are clearly brought out in this chapter, as may

[1] This development is briefly noticed by J. Denis, "Denys d'Halicar-nasse, Jugement sur Lysias" (*Faculté des Lettres de Caen, Bulletin Mensuel,* 1890), p. 181, "ces minutieuses analyses sont pourtant plus instructives à beaucoup d'égards que les observations précédentes. Ce n'est pas dans le *Jugement sur Lysias* qu'on les rencontre."
[2] Cf. my article, "Dionysius of Halicarnassus and the Peripatetic Mean of Style", *C.P.* xxxiii (1938), p. 265.

be seen from the interjections which appear between the examples
he examines—"and this is not enough for him, but in the very next
period...and then without even a brief interval he adds...if he
were moderate up to this point he would be bearable, but he will not
forbear...and then, just as though he had not said anything of the
kind, he will swamp us with a host of parisoses". It is also interesting
to observe that Dionysius was sufficiently open-minded to acknowledge that in the later speeches of Isocrates these "puerile figures"
became less frequent; time, he adds caustically, evidently brought
wisdom in its train.[1]

Further evidence of this type of analysis is to be found in the
concluding chapter of the essay, where Dionysius subjects parts of
the *Trapeziticus* (his παράδειγμα of a δικανικὸς λόγος) to detailed
criticism. Of the four passages there commented upon, the last may
suffice as an example.[2] The sentence ὥστε πίστεις τε ⟨τὰς⟩ μεγίστας
αὐτῷ δεδωκὼς εἴη καὶ τὴν ἀρχὴν ἔτι μείζω πεποιηκὼς ἧς εἶχε πρότερον
καὶ τὴν ἀδελφὴν τὴν ἐμὴν γυναῖκα τῷ ἑαυτοῦ υἱεῖ εἰληφώς is censured
on the ground of its parallelisms in sound, δεδωκώς... πεποιηκώς...
εἰληφώς, and ἀρχήν...ἀδελφήν. Admittedly this and the similar
criticisms in c. 14 are fairly obvious to any reader of Isocrates,
though perhaps not every critic would be quite so deeply offended;
but from the point of view of development in critical exposition
these chapters are of considerable significance, for in them Dionysius
abandons generalities, makes closer contact with the actual text, and
supports his statements with evidence.

In the last essay of the first volume of the work on the orators, the
De Isaeo, the same general plan is adopted as in the two preceding
essays. The little that is known about the life of Isaeus is first given
(c. 1), and followed by a statement, which strikes the keynote of the
study, on the great similarity between Isaeus and Lysias (c. 2);
several chapters are next devoted to the style of Isaeus, viewed in
relation to that of Lysias (cc. 3–12) and Demosthenes (c. 13); next we
have criticism of Isaeus' treatment of subject-matter (cc. 14–16), and
then a speech of Isaeus is cited by way of a παράδειγμα (cc. 17–18);

[1] c. 14 *sub fin.* (= 1, 76) οἱ μέντοι γε ἐπὶ τελευτῇ τοῦ βίου γραφέντες
λόγοι ἧττόν εἰσι μειρακιώδεις, ὡς ἂν οἶμαι τελείαν ἀπειληφότες τὴν φρόνησιν
παρὰ τοῦ χρόνου.
[2] c. 20 (= 1, 91).

finally, brief accounts of the "lesser" orators (Gorgias, Alcidamas, Theodorus, Anaximenes, Antiphon, Thrasymachus, Polycrates, Critias, Zoilus) serve as an appendix to the first volume of the work.

Dionysius' aim, of course, in presenting this study, was the same as in his earlier essays, namely, to give advice, for purposes of imitation, on the standard models. It is noticeable, however, that he does not lay such constant stress on this principle of μίμησις as in previous essays; it does not dominate the study, in which Dionysius is occupied with the difficult task of expressing his views on an orator whose characteristics are by no means so striking or easily defined as those of Lysias and Isocrates. In fact, throughout the essay, the only indications of practical rhetorical purpose are to be seen in those passages in which Isaeus is criticised as being too obvious in his use of the devices of rhetoric, whereas Lysias lets art conceal art.[1]

With this relaxing of the tension of immediate practical purpose, the signs of rhetorical method also to some extent diminish. There is in the *De Isaeo* very little actual application of the code of virtues of style; in fact after a brief opening sentence in which Dionysius remarks that "the style of Isaeus is pure, accurate, lucid, consists of ordinary words, is vivid, brief, convincing, appropriate to the case, compact, and suited to forensic oratory no less than the style of Lysias",[2] mechanical criticism according to a series of tests entirely disappears. Rhetorical subdivisions occasionally persist; in c. 3 and elsewhere[3] we encounter the now familiar divisions of σύνθεσις and σχήματα, while Dionysius' remarks on Isaeus' treatment of his subject-matter in c. 3 are again couched in technical phraseology. If the essay be judged as a whole, however, it is hard to resist the

[1] E.g. c. 7 (= 1, 100) οὐ λέληθεν, ὅτι ἐστὶ ῥητορικόν. c. 8 (= 1, 101) παρ' ᾧ μὲν ἀφελέστερον...παρ' ᾧ δὲ ῥητορικώτερον. c. 9 (= 1, 103) τὸ γάρ... οὐδεὶς ἂν εἴποι ῥήτορος εἶναι...τὸ δ' Ἰσαίου πεποιῆσθαι ῥητορικῶς καὶ κεκαλλιλογῆσθαι σεμνότερον ἅπαντες ἂν φήσειαν. c. 11 (= 1, 106) οὐ λανθάνοντα ὅτι πέπλασται ῥητορικῇ τέχνῃ. The principle of art concealing art, strongly emphasised by Aristotle (*Rhet.* III, 2, 4; 7, 10 etc.), was a favourite in the rhetorical schools; cf. D'Alton, *op. cit.* pp. 133-4.

[2] c. 2 *init.* (= 1, 94) καθαρὰ μὲν καὶ ἀκριβὴς καὶ σαφὴς κυρία τε καὶ ἐναργὴς καὶ σύντομος, πρὸς δὲ τούτοις πιθανή τε καὶ πρέπουσα τοῖς ὑποκειμένοις στρογγύλη τε καὶ δικανικὴ οὐχ ἧττόν ἐστιν ἡ Ἰσαίου λέξις τῆς Λυσίου κ.τ.λ.

[3] E.g. c. 12, c. 13 *sub fin.*

conclusion that Dionysius has made less use of mechanical aids to criticism than in preceding essays. Certainly he has made an honest attempt to capture the elusive personality of Isaeus in those chapters in which he compares him with other writers; and it is to the merits of these chapters, which set the essay ahead of its predecessors in point of exposition, that we may now turn.

Comparative criticism in the *De Isaeo* shows a great advance on anything previously attempted. In the *De Imitatione* it had been mechanical and frigid, in the *De Lysia* it had been confined to a very few remarks, in the *De Isocrate* it had not improved very considerably, being restricted to general observations without illustration and based on the stylistic system; in the *De Isaeo* it is a recurring feature throughout. It is in fact true to say that Dionysius scarcely mentions Isaeus in this essay without comparing or contrasting him with Lysias or Demosthenes. In cc. 3 and 4 he sets forth in general terms the difference between Isaeus and Lysias. Lysias is simple and true to character, is more natural in composition and unaffected in his use of figures; his style is amply endowed with pleasantness and charm. Isaeus, on the other hand, is more artistic, more precise, more elaborate in composition, and diversifies his style with a great variety of figures. The style of Lysias may be compared with early paintings, which reveal no subtlety in the mixing of colours, but are correct in outline and derive charm from this simplicity; that of Isaeus is like later paintings which are less well defined in their outlines, but exhibit a greater perfection of detail, and derive their effect from their subtle interplay of light and shade and their variety of colour effects.[1] Finally, the speeches of Isaeus (and Demosthenes), even when they deal with honest and straightforward issues, are suspected because of their abundance of artifice, whereas those of Lysias (and Isocrates), even when they are anything but honest and straightforward, arouse no suspicion of double-dealing.[2]

Nor is this comparative criticism confined to such general remarks; Dionysius proceeds to demonstrate by illustration. In cc. 5 and 6 he

---

[1] Cf. Cicero, *Brutus*, § 70 "Similis in pictura ratio est; in qua Zeuxim et Polygnotum et Timanthem et eorum, qui non sunt usi plus quam quattuor coloribus, formas et liniamenta laudamus; at in Aetione Nicomacho Protogene Apelle iam perfecta sunt omnia."

[2] c. 4 *sub fin.* (= I, 97).

quotes a proem of Isaeus (Ὑπὲρ Εὐμάθους), and a proem of Lysias (Περὶ Φερενίκου); in c. 7 he then proceeds to give his analysis and comment. The same plan is followed in c. 8 where a passage of Lysias (frag. LXII, S.) and a passage of Isaeus (frag. X, 1, S.) are cited, and followed in c. 9 by the comments of the critic, as before. So in c. 10 passages of Lysias (Πρὸς Ἀρχεβιάδην = frag. XIX, S.) and Isaeus (frag. VII, 1, S.) are quoted, and in c. 11 subjected to analysis and criticism. There is also some excellent comparative criticism in cc. 12 and 13 where Isaeus and Demosthenes are compared from the point of view of their use of disjointed sentences and rhetorical questions. Here Dionysius has seized upon an essential feature common to the two orators, and has brought it out well by his illustrations. In his comparative criticism therefore, and his greater readiness to illustrate his remarks, he has improved very considerably on his earlier work.

There is also in the *De Isaeo* considerably more analysis than in any of the previous essays. In the *De Imitatione* and *De Lysia* no analysis was attempted; in the *De Isocrate* its appearance in cc. 14 and 20 marked a distinct advance; in the *De Isaeo* it reappears in cc. 7, 9, 11 and 13. Dionysius' method is to break up a given passage of Lysias or Isaeus into its component sentences, and then to comment separately on each sentence. As the aim of his study is to compare and contrast Isaeus with Lysias, his comments tend to be of a somewhat general nature; he is contented to state that a given sentence of Lysias is simple and unaffected, whereas another of Isaeus is artificial and involved.[1] To Dionysius' readers, of course, Greek was a familiar spoken language, and they would no doubt at once have endorsed Dionysius' remarks that one sentence was, and another was not, in the manner of an ordinary individual; but modern readers, who have to be content with the unsatisfactory medium of the written word, often wonder why a certain word or phrase is "artificial rather than natural",[2] and would appreciate a deeper analysis.

---

[1] E.g. c. 7 *init.* (= 1, 100) παρὰ Λυσίᾳ μὲν...φυσικῶς πως εἴρηται καὶ ἀφελῶς...παρὰ δὲ Ἰσαίῳ κατεσκεύασται τὸ δοκοῦν εἶναι ἀφελές κ.τ.λ.

[2] *Ib.* ἥ τε γὰρ προπέτεια καὶ ἡ ἀδικία καὶ τὸ πρὸς τὰ Εὐμάθους πράγματα προσελθεῖν πεποιημένοις μᾶλλον ἔοικεν ἢ αὐτοφυέσι. Cf. J. Denis, *op. cit.* pp. 184-5, especially p. 185 "Quoiqu'il soit assez téméraire et qu'il puisse paraître impertinent de disputer sur le grec avec un grec de naissance et

It is the introduction in two passages of the *De Isaeo* of a deeper analysis that marks the beginning of a further advance in critical exposition. In criticising an author, the critic may confine himself to general observations, and these may be true enough and well enough said; but if he takes the trouble to illustrate those observations, he may be considered to have performed his task as critic more satisfactorily still. If he goes farther, and analyses separate passages to explain his views, then he has made a real attempt to communicate his reactions to the reader. Comparative criticism, too, will add to his powers of exposition. But if he proceeds, after explaining and analysing, to show the reader how he himself would rewrite the passage, then he has reached a very high standard of analytical criticism.[1] This is exactly the procedure which Dionysius adopts on two occasions in this essay. There had been a slight indication of this method once in the *De Isocrate*;[2] but it is in the *De Isaeo* that it begins to make itself felt as a powerful aid to critical expression. Quoting the sentence[3] τριηραρχοῦντος γὰρ ⟨μου⟩ ἐπὶ Κηφισοδότου ἄρχοντος καὶ λόγου ἀπαγγελθέντος πρὸς τοὺς οἰκείους, ὡς ἄρα τετελευτηκὼς εἴην ἐν τῇ ναυμαχίᾳ, οὔσης μοι παρακαταθήκης παρ' Εὐμάθει τούτῳ...κ.τ.λ. Dionysius objects to its lack of simplicity in structure, referring to λόγου ἀπαγγελθέντος πρὸς τοὺς οἰκείους, ὡς ἄρα τετελευτηκὼς εἴην ἐν τῇ ναυμαχίᾳ and οὔσης μοι παρακαταθήκης; but it is only when he rewrites the sentence as follows: ὅτε γὰρ ἐτριηράρχουν καὶ ἀπηγγέλη τοῖς ἐνθάδε, ὡς ἄρα τετελευτηκὼς εἴην, ἔχων μου παρακαταθήκην Εὐμάθης οὑτοσί...κ.τ.λ. that we see for certain that it is the accumulation of genitive absolutes to which he objects; and as a result of this recasting his criticism becomes much more illuminating and instructive. Similarly when Dionysius objects to the sentence πολλῶν μοι καὶ δυσκόλων συμπιπτόντων οὐχ ἡγούμην δεῖν κατοκνῆσαι δι' ὑμῶν πειρᾶσθαι τυγχάνειν τῶν δικαίων on the ground

d'éducation, je prendrai encore un exemple parmi les trois que cite Denys pour faire sentir ce que sa critique de détail a de minutieux à la fois et de peu sûr ou du moins d'impénétrable pour nous."

[1] I am here considering analytical criticism only; spontaneous expression may, of course, surpass even the most detailed analysis. Cf. p. 104 below.

[2] c. 20 (= I, 91).   [3] c. 7 *sub fin.* (= I, 101).

that no ordinary individual would speak in that way, and rewrites τοσούτων γέ μοι συμπιπτόντων δυσκόλων ἐφ' ὑμᾶς ἠνάγκασμαι καταφυγεῖν, ἵνα τῶν δικαίων τύχω δι' ὑμῶν he gives the reader a much clearer idea of his opinion of the artificiality and affectation therein involved.[1]

Finally, there is recognised in the *De Isaeo*, for the first time, the possibility of the influence of one stylist upon another. In each of the previous essays the possible influences on an author's style, and his possible effect upon the styles of others are quite disregarded; but here we have emphasis repeatedly laid on the fact that in certain ways Isaeus paved the way for Demosthenes.[2] Dionysius sees in Isaeus the first-beginnings of that abruptness of utterance, that masterly use of sudden, unexpected questions, so disconcerting to the adversary, and that curiously contorted method of expression so characteristic of Demosthenes.[3] In the *De Isaeo* the canvas which is fully unfolded in the *De Demosthene* is for the first time revealed; Isaeus takes on a new significance, as he plays an important part in the historical development of Greek prose. In short, there is now added to the critic's merits what may be termed the cultivation of a historical point of view in matters of style.[4]

It may be convenient at this point to look back and assess the results of the investigation into the first four essays. That there has been a considerable improvement in the critic's power of exposition seems undeniable. His greater readiness to illustrate is noticed in

[1] c. 11 *sub fin.* (= 1, 107).

[2] c. 3 πηγή τις ὄντως ἐστὶ τῆς Δημοσθένους δυνάμεως. c. 7 οὐ μακρὰν ἀπέχει τῆς Δημοσθένους κατασκευῆς. c. 13 Δημοσθένης δὲ ὁ παρὰ τουτουὶ τὰς ἀφορμὰς λαβών. *Ib. sub fin.* πολλὰ γὰρ ἄν τις εὕροι τῶν Ἰσαίου...ἐοικότα ...τῇ Δημοσθένους δεινότητι. c. 16 ἐν γὰρ δὴ τούτοις οὐχ ἧττόν ἐστι φανερὸς τῇ Δημοσθένους τέχνῃ τὰς ἀφορμὰς δεδωκώς. c. 20 ὅτι μοι δοκεῖ τῆς Δημοσθένους δεινότητος...τὰ σπέρματα καὶ τὰς ἀρχὰς οὗτος ὁ ἀνὴρ παρασχεῖν.

[3] Cf. especially c. 13.

[4] Egger's remark (in Desrousseaux-Egger, *Denys d'Halicarnasse, Jugement sur Lysias*, Paris 1890, p. xx): "ce qui leur manque le plus, si nous nous plaçons au point de vue des exigences modernes, c'est ce qui manque à la critique de Denys et à la critique ancienne, c'est le sentiment historique" is true of the *De Lysia*, but not of the *De Isaeo* and some of the later essays.

the *De Isocrate* and is particularly evident in the *De Isaeo*. His use of the method of analysis appears for the first time in the *De Isocrate*, and is continued in the *De Isaeo*, with the important addition of the recasting of two passages. His comparative criticism was frigid and mechanical in the *De Imitatione*, and hardly better in the *De Isocrate*, but is improved beyond measure in the *De Isaeo*. His mental activity has considerably increased, for in the *De Imitatione*, the *De Lysia*, and even in the *De Isocrate* he is hampered by the system of virtues of style, whereas in the *De Isaeo* he is a much more independent investigator. Finally, there is noticeable an improvement in outlook; for when he began Dionysius was too prone to treat Greek writers as separate individuals, whereas he now sees that there may be interrelation, and that there is such a thing as the evolution of the art of prose style. In short, even though these essays lie under the shadow of the rhetorical school with its insistence on imitation, its technical terminology and its subdivisions, there is a marked move away from the mechanical use of rhetorical resources towards a freer and more independent type of exposition.

CHAPTER IV

The essays of the middle period—the first letter to
Ammaeus, on Demosthenes, on literary composition,
and the letter to Pompeius

THE first letter to Ammaeus does not properly belong to the sphere of literary criticism; it deals rather with a point of literary history, and its methods are accordingly those of the historian rather than those of the critic. The whole question involved is one of chronology, and it is only the result of the investigation which has any importance for the student of literary criticism in the narrow sense. There is in this essay little or no expression of opinion upon questions of style, and it therefore stands apart in this respect from those essays which have hitherto been considered; on the other hand, as has already been observed,[1] the subject of the letter shows that Dionysius was still proceeding along the lines taken for the first time in the *De Isaeo*, and was still bent on discovering the various influences which might, or might not, have affected an author's style. As an interesting study in scientific method it merits a brief consideration.

It is worthy of mention, first, that Dionysius had already had occasion to tackle a similar problem in an earlier essay (*De Lysia,* c. 12), though the introduction of the chronological study had there been incidental, and did not, as here, represent the main issue. In the *De Lysia* passage, Dionysius had been concerned to prove that two speeches Περὶ τῆς Ἰφικράτους Εἰκόνος and Περὶ τῆς Προδοσίας, commonly ascribed in his day to Lysias, were not the work of Lysias at all. He had expressed a conviction that this was so, not only because the speeches failed to exhibit the characteristic charm of Lysias, but also because the ascription of them to him raised chronological difficulties.[2] To prove his point Dionysius had

---

[1] Above, p. 34.
[2] *De Lysia,* c. 12 (= I, 20) μάλιστα δ' ἐγένετό μοι καταφανὴς ὅτι οὐχ ὑπ' ἐκείνου τοῦ ῥήτορος ἐγράφη, τοὺς χρόνους ἀναλογισαμένῳ.

assumed that Lysias lived to the age of 80, and died in the archonship of Nicon (379–8 B.C.) or Nausinicus (378–7 B.C.); and mentioning that the first of the two speeches was later than the archonship of Alcisthenes (372–1 B.C.) he had concluded that this speech must have been at least seven years too late to have been composed by Lysias. With regard to the second speech, Dionysius had declared that it belonged to the period of the Social War (357–5 B.C.) and was therefore at least 20 years later than the death of Lysias.

In the *Epistula ad Ammaeum* 1 Dionysius is equally clear and logical and also goes into greater detail. He first of all gives the dates of Demosthenes' birth and of the delivery of twelve of his speeches which preceded the Olynthian War (c. 4). Then he briefly outlines the life of Aristotle (c. 5), and establishes the sequence of some of his works by the methods now applied by scholars to his own essays (c. 6). Having thus shown that the *Rhetoric* is a mature work, Dionysius proves from the reference to the Olynthian War in *Rhet.* III, 10, § 7 that it is later than 349 B.C.; his evidence for the dating of the war is drawn from Philochorus. Clearly, therefore, he argues, Demosthenes had composed at least a dozen speeches before Aristotle could have published his *Rhetoric* (cc. 7–9). Repeating his procedure, Dionysius next dates twelve more speeches of Demosthenes, which, he declares, were composed before 339 B.C. (c. 10); he then proves conclusively from passages of Philochorus and the *De Corona* that the reference to Philip's request for a passage through Thebes in *Rhet.* II, 23, § 6 is to the events of that year; yet a second series of speeches, therefore, was written before Aristotle's *Rhetoric* had appeared (c. 11). Finally, Dionysius attempts to prove that the *De Corona* itself was composed before the *Rhetoric* (c. 12); but here his evidence is not so satisfactory; for it is very improbable that ἡ περὶ Δημοσθένους δίκη in *Rhetoric* II, 23, § 3 refers to the case against Aeschines.[1] However, Dionysius has sufficiently refuted the theory of his contemporary and in so doing has revealed himself as a master of clear argument and logical exposition.

It is now time to resume the main line of the present study and to consider an equally important contribution to the criticism of Demosthenes, the *De admiranda vi dicendi in Demosthene*. This

     [1] Cf. Cope-Sandys *ad loc.*

essay, as has been already pointed out,¹ falls into two distinct sections, separated by the production of the *De Compositione Verborum*.

In the first section of the *De Demosthene*, it is clear from several of the critic's remarks that his study is, like the preceding essays, designed as an aid to μίμησις, particularly with regard to forensic and deliberative oratory. So Isocrates is criticised because he lacks emotional power, and it is most essential that a pleader before the people or in a law court should possess this power;² he lacks spirit, too, which is "essential in forensic oratory",³ and the compactness of the forensic style.⁴ Similarly Thucydides frequently, but Demosthenes only rarely lacks lucidity, "which is the first essential in forensic speeches".⁵ The concluding passage of Plato's *Menexenus* is found good, but not ἐναγώνιος, and therefore, presumably, not a fully satisfactory model.⁶

There is also evidence in the *De Demosthene* of the use of the rhetorical system. The virtues of style appear occasionally in full array, as in c. 13 (on Lysias), and in c. 18 (on Isocrates), though it cannot be said that they dominate the treatment of the subject. Use is made, however, for the first time (in these essays), of the three types of style. Dionysius' expressed aim in cc. 1–33 is to prove the superiority of Demosthenes as a model to the other important writers, and in order to do this he classifies the outstanding writers of Greek prose according to the three types, plain, middle, and grand. Gorgias and Thucydides appear as representatives of the grand style (c. 1), Lysias as the representative of the plain style (c. 2), and Thrasymachus, Isocrates, and Plato as the best exponents of the middle style (cc. 3–7). Demosthenes is regarded as superior

¹ Above, pp. 31 ff.
² *De Dem.* c. 18 (= 1, 166) ἦν δὲ ἄρα πάντων ἰσχυρότατον τῷ μέλλοντι πείθειν δῆμον ἢ δικαστήριον, ἐπὶ τὰ πάθη τοὺς ἀκροατὰς ἀγαγεῖν.
³ *Ib.* c. 20 (= 1, 170) πνεύματός τε, οὗ μάλιστα δεῖ τοῖς ἐναγωνίοις λόγοις, ἐλαχίστην ἔχουσα μοῖραν (*sc.* ἡ τοῦ Ἰσοκράτους διάλεκτος).
⁴ c. 18 (= 1, 166).
⁵ c. 10 (= 1, 149) οὔτε τὸ σαφὲς ἐκβέβηκεν (*sc.* ὁ Δημοσθένης), οὗ πρώτου τοῖς ἐναγωνίοις λόγοις δεῖ.
⁶ c. 30 (= 1, 197) πλὴν ὅτι πολιτικόν γε τὸ σχῆμα αὐτῆς ἐστιν, οὐκ ἐναγώνιον.

to each of these writers because of his ability to employ any of the three styles, and to reach an extremely high standard of expression in each (cc. 8–33). Naturally, this treatment gives a very formal appearance to the essay as a whole; and it is also responsible for considerable artificiality, for writers like Isocrates and Plato, who are incongruously grouped together within the middle "type", are spoken of as though they were armed with two quite separate and distinct styles, either of which they could pick up or lay aside at will. Isocrates is regarded as employing the artless, unadorned style of Lysias for purposes of exposition, and the ornate and magnificent style of Gorgias for purposes of emotional effect.[1] So Plato is highly praised when he uses the simple style, which he has cultivated to perfection, but severely censured when he adopts the high-flown style and renders his meaning obscure.[2] For this rigid confinement of individual authors within the three fixed categories of style (whatever their ultimate origin) we have to thank the rhetorical schools; as a means of encouraging the young rhetorician to perceive the differences between styles and to master each in turn for the purposes of argument and appeal, this method may have been of considerable service; but when used as a basis for literary criticism it merely hampers freedom of appreciation and expression, and tempts the critic to forget how personal and individual a thing is style.

However, the merits which result from the employment of this method are immeasurably greater than the faults; for the plan is responsible for a great deal of comparative criticism of the most illuminating kind. To bring out the great predominance of the comparative method throughout this first portion of the *De Demosthene* it is necessary to summarise the whole argument of the

[1] *De Dem.* c. 4 (= 1, 135) καὶ εἰς μὲν τὸ διδάξαι τὸν ἀκροατὴν σαφέστατα ὅ τι βούλοιτο, τὴν ἁπλῆν καὶ ἀκόσμητον ἑρμηνείαν ἐπιτηδεύει τὴν Λυσίου, εἰς δὲ τὸ καταπλήξασθαι τῷ κάλλει τῶν ὀνομάτων σεμνότητά τε καὶ μεγαληγορίαν περιθεῖναι τοῖς πράγμασι τὴν ἐπίθετον καὶ κατεσκευασμένην φράσιν τῶν περὶ Γοργίαν ἐκμέμακται.
[2] *Ib.* c. 5 (= 1, 136–7) ὅταν μὲν οὖν τὴν ἰσχνὴν καὶ ἀφελῆ καὶ ἀποίητον ἐπιτηδεύῃ φράσιν, ἐκτόπως ἡδεῖά ἐστι καὶ φιλάνθρωπος...ὅταν δὲ εἰς τὴν περιττολογίαν καὶ τὸ καλλιεπεῖν, ὃ πολλάκις εἴωθε ποιεῖν, ἄμετρον ὁρμὴν λάβῃ, πολλῷ χείρων ἑαυτῆς γίνεται.

first 33 chapters. Dionysius begins (in the text as it stands to-day) by giving two examples of the grand style—passages from Gorgias and Thucydides—together with a very brief sketch of the characteristics of that type (c. 1). He then names the chief exponents of the plain style, among whom Lysias stands first; but as he has already dealt fully with Lysias he proceeds to emphasise the differences between his style and that of the "grand" stylist *par excellence*, Thucydides. "The style of Thucydides has power to shock the mind, the style of Lysias to gratify it; the one can rally and brace it, the other relax and soothe it; the one can work upon the emotions, the other inspire tranquil sentiment. Moreover, it is a characteristic of Thucydides' style to insist and drive the point home, of Lysias' to mislead and to conceal the facts. Innovation and venturesomeness are inseparable from the historian's character, as are cautiousness and avoidance of risk from the orator's."[1] Lysias and Thucydides, in short, are poles— or rather, as Dionysius says, an octave—apart (c. 2). The representatives of the middle style are next considered and an example of the style given from Thrasymachus (c. 3). An example from Isocrates is not adduced, as he has already been discussed; but the contrast of his style with that of Lysias is recapitulated from the second chapter of the *De Isocrate* (c. 4). Three chapters follow on the style of Plato (cc. 5–7), and then the superior versatility of Demosthenes is proclaimed (c. 8). From this point onwards we have a series of comparisons and contrasts systematically arranged.

First, Demosthenes is compared and contrasted with Thucydides (cc. 9–10); Dionysius finds a certain resemblance between them in their desire to avoid the simple, natural manner of expression and in their efforts to render their style striking and unusual. By analysing passages of the *Third Philippic* and the *Midias* he shows that the element of distinction is there obtained by a deliberate abnormality of arrangement. "What is it," he asks of one

---

[1] I, 131 ἡ μὲν γὰρ καταπλήξασθαι δύναται τὴν διάνοιαν, ἡ δὲ ἡδῦναι, καὶ ἡ μὲν συστρέψαι καὶ συντεῖναι τὸν νοῦν, ἡ δὲ ἀνεῖναι καὶ μαλάξαι, καὶ εἰς πάθος ἐκείνη προαγαγεῖν, εἰς δὲ ἦθος αὕτη καταστῆσαι. πλὴν ἀλλὰ καὶ τὸ μὲν βιάσασθαι καὶ προσαναγκάσαι τι τῆς Θουκυδίδου λέξεως ἴδιον, τὸ δ' ἀπατῆσαι καὶ κλέψαι τὰ πράγματα τῆς Λυσίου. καὶ ἡ μὲν νεωτεροποιΐα καὶ τὸ τολμηρὸν τῆς τοῦ συγγραφέως οἰκεῖον ἰδέας, ἡ δ' ἀσφάλεια καὶ τὸ ἀκίνδυνον τῆς τοῦ ῥήτορος.

passage,[1] "that upsets the natural expression? It is the insertion of a second idea, or phrase, or whatever we should term it, before the first is concluded, and the addition of a third even before the second is complete; then, after the conclusion of the third, the completion of the second and, on top of all, the resumption of the first after a long interval, when the mind no longer expects it." Demosthenes and Thucydides do, however, differ in one important respect: Thucydides uses this method of obtaining distinction so unsparingly as to become obscure, whereas Demosthenes always aims at the golden mean and, as a result, does not violate the essential principles of perspicuity and propriety.[2]

Next, the style of Demosthenes is compared and contrasted with that of Lysias (cc. 11–13); and in certain passages the critic discovers an even more marked resemblance than that between Demosthenes and Thucydides. Resorting to the system of virtues employed in the *De Lysia* he asks if the purity, accuracy, lucidity, brevity, and the remaining qualities of Lysias (exemplified by a passage of the κατὰ Τίσιδος) are not also present in the speech of Demosthenes κατὰ Κόνωνος, a portion of which he quotes. "If the authorship of these speeches were not revealed by their titles," he declares,[3] "I imagine few of us would easily distinguish that of Demosthenes from that of Lysias." The great difference between these writers, Dionysius concludes, lies in the vigour shown by Demosthenes in his proofs, as contrasted with the indistinctness and feebleness of Lysias. Lysias' charm carries him "like a breeze from the south" through prologue and narrative, but deserts him in the later stages of the speech; there, too, he lacks that power and intensity which Demosthenes does not sacrifice when he adopts a plain and unadorned style.

Finally Dionysius turns to the middle type of style and first gives a few examples of it from Demosthenes (*or.* XIX, 258, *or.* XXIII, 65, and *or.* XX, 68), and defends it as the most satisfactory of the three, and the best adapted to audiences (cc. 14–15). He then proceeds to study a passage of the *De Pace* of Isocrates, who, together with Plato, is his accepted representative of this χαρακτήρ. Here again

---

[1] c. 9 (= I, 147), of *Midias* § 69.
[2] c. 10 (= I, 148–9); Peripatetic influence is again noticeable here, cf. *C.P.* XXXIII (1938), p. 264.
[3] I, 156.

he reverts for a while to his system of virtues, and remarks upon the
purity, accuracy, and lucidity of the style, as well as its stateliness,
dignity, and general beauty of form; there is much, however, which
is far from praiseworthy, for Isocrates has no sense of brevity, no
compactness, no daring expressions, no force, no intensity, no power
to stir, no variety. His general conclusions are then supported by
analysis. Of one passage he makes the excellent observation "The
style should have been harsh and bitter and should have struck home
like a blow; as it is, it is soft and even and glides quietly through the
ear like oil, seeking to bewitch and charm."[1] Moreover, he adds,
puerile figures, frigid antitheses, and the like, greatly detract from
the effect and render the speech "one long antithesis"; "diversions,
changes, varieties are nowhere to be found".[2]

So the scene is laid for the triumphant entry of Demosthenes, a
passage of whose *Third Olynthiac* (on a subject similar to that of the
De Pace) is quoted. Few critics, I think, would differ from the
enthusiastic verdict of Dionysius. "Who would refuse to acknowledge", he enquires, "the complete superiority of this style to that
of Isocrates? Demosthenes has expressed the subject-matter with
greater nobility and magnificence, has clothed the ideas with a
finer style, and brought them out in a more concise, compact, and
finished fashion; he has shown greater power and a sturdier strength,
and avoided those frigid, childish figures in which the other indulges
to excess; but it is in movement, action, emotional effect, that he is
completely and absolutely superior."[3] It is in the course of this
excellent comparison that Dionysius pens the celebrated passage in
which he describes the totally different effects which the works of
Isocrates and Demosthenes have upon him. "When I read a
speech of Isocrates," he says, "I become serious in spirit, and
experience great mental calm, like those who listen to the pipes
during libations or to Dorian or enharmonic melodies. But when
I take up one of Demosthenes' speeches, I am entranced and borne

[1] c. 20 (= I, 171) τραχεῖαν γὰρ ἔδει καὶ πικρὰν εἶναι καὶ πληγῇ τι
παραπλήσιον ποιεῖν· ἡ δ᾽ ἔστιν ὑγρὰ καὶ ὁμαλὴ καὶ ὥσπερ ἔλαιον ἀψοφητὶ
διὰ τῆς ἀκοῆς ῥέουσα, θέλγειν γέ τοι καὶ ἡδύνειν ζητοῦσα τὴν ἀκοήν.
[2] *Ib.* τό τε πρᾶγμα ὅλον ἐστὶν ἀντίθεσις, and (I, 172) τροπαὶ δὲ καὶ
μεταβολαὶ καὶ ποικιλίαι σχημάτων...οὐδαμοῦ.
[3] c. 21 (= I, 175).

BLT 5

hither and thither, experiencing one emotion after another, distrust, anxiety, fear, contempt, hatred, pity, benevolence, anger, envy, every emotion in fact that is wont to dominate the human mind. I seem to be no whit different from those who perform rites of initiation.... If then we, who are so far removed in time, and are not concerned about the issue, are thus swayed and mastered, and borne whithersoever the speech carries us, how must the Athenians and the Greeks in general have felt when their living interests were at stake, and when the orator himself, at the height of his fame, revealed his own personal experience and laid bare the inmost feelings of his soul?"[1] With this magnificent tribute, perhaps the finest in his works, Dionysius draws his comparison to a close.

Having thus established the superiority of Demosthenes over Isocrates, Dionysius now turns to Plato (cc. 23 ff.). It is, however, important to notice here that he is not merely actuated by a desire to show the superiority of Demosthenes; he is driven by a strong impulse to refute the extravagant admirers of Plato who sought to elevate him as a model beyond all orators as well as philosophers. It is in the light of this expressed aim of Dionysius that the criticisms of Plato which follow must be studied; and the severity of his censure must in part at least be attributed to his indignation at this far-fetched claim of certain contemporary philosophers.[2]

However, true to his conception of the critic's function—to ascertain the truth and express it without fear or favour—Dionysius promises a fair treatment. "I did not approve", he says,[3] "of the method adopted by some writers of selecting the worst passages from all his (Plato's) works and then contrasting with these the finest of Demosthenes; it seemed to me just to place together passages from the most reputable works of both, and to decide which

---

[1] c. 22 (= I, 176–7).

[2] c. 23 (= I, 178) καὶ μάλιστα ἐπεί τινες ἀξιοῦσι πάντων αὐτὸν ἀποφαίνειν φιλοσόφων τε καὶ ῥητόρων ἑρμηνεῦσαι τὰ πράγματα δαιμονιώτατον παρακελεύονταί τε ἡμῖν ὅρῳ καὶ κανόνι χρῆσθαι καθαρῶν ἅμα καὶ ἰσχυρῶν λόγων τούτῳ τῷ ἀνδρί. The allusion is possibly to some of the more ardent disciples of Poseidonius, though this reverence for Plato was common in Cicero's day; cf. especially *Brutus*, § 121 with the present passage.

[3] *Ib.* (= I, 179).

was superior." This is indeed a fair promise; and we recall the similar statement of procedure made earlier in the essay, in which Dionysius said "I will now proceed to deal with those passages of both writers (viz. Isocrates and Plato) which appear best, and contrast with them passages of Demosthenes *written on the same subjects*, in order that the aims and achievements of the authors may become clear when they are subjected to the most thorough test *in similar works.*"[1] But when Dionysius (c. 23) selects the *Menexenus*, and pits it against the most celebrated passage of the *De Corona*, he lays himself open to the objection that he has not really chosen "similar works"; for the *Menexenus*, even if it is genuine Plato, is not a forensic, or even a deliberative, oration, and certainly has little or no affinity with the *De Corona*. Dionysius himself seems half-conscious of the fact that he has chosen works of a different character when he admits that the *Menexenus* has σχῆμα πολιτικόν...οὐκ ἐναγώνιον. It would, of course, be almost impossible to find a ὅμοιον ἔργον of Plato, for the *Apology*, as he says, "never even saw the doors of a law court".[2] However, apart from the unfortunate choice of a work which was in all probability merely a parody,[3] Dionysius carries out his examination carefully enough. His chief objections are to frigid antitheses, redundancy, inaccurate use of language, commonplace ideas, and general lack of dignity and elevation. Contrasting with the *Menexenus* the most celebrated passage of the *De Corona* (§§ 199–209, containing the "Marathon oath"), Dionysius concludes that the works of Demosthenes and Plato differ "as widely as the weapons of war from those of display, as reality from a mere image, as bodies strengthened by exercise in the sun from those that are inactive in the shadows".[4] From a strictly rhetorical standpoint his claim is reasonable; but the last purpose that Plato was likely to serve was that of the rhetorician.

---

[1] c. 16 *sub fin.* τὴν ἀκριβεστάτην βάσανον ἐπὶ τῶν ὁμοίων ἔργων λαβοῦσαι.

[2] I, 180 δικαστηρίου μὲν ἢ ἀγορᾶς οὐδὲ θύρας ἰδών.

[3] See the thorough investigation of L. Meridier in his introduction to the Budé edition of the *Menexenus* (*Platon, Oeuvres* v, Paris, 1931), and literature there quoted.

[4] c. 32 (= I, 201) ὅσῳ διαλλάττει πολεμιστήρια μὲν ὅπλα πομπευτηρίων, ἀληθιναὶ δὲ ὄψεις εἰδώλων, ἐν ἡλίῳ δὲ καὶ πόνοις τεθραμμένα σώματα τῶν σκιὰς καὶ ῥᾳστώνας διωκόντων.

Of the series of comparisons and contrasts made in the *De Demosthene*, that between Demosthenes and Plato is the least successful; the others are models of their kind, and it can hardly be denied that the comparative criticism of this essay is carried out on a much wider scale and more successfully than in any of the earlier essays.[1] It now remains to consider the further merits and defects of the essay in relation to those of the studies which preceded it.

It will have been realised from the foregoing summary of the *De Demosthene* that it contains abundant illustration and analysis. It is noteworthy that throughout the thirty-three chapters only a few examples of illustration without subsequent analysis appear. The passages of Gorgias and Thucydides which illustrate the grand style and that of Thrasymachus which illustrates the middle are not analysed —nor indeed does the reader expect them to be—neither are the passages of Plato in c. 7 and Demosthenes in c. 14, though here it would have been useful to know exactly what Dionysius found objectionable in the Plato passage and what specific characteristics of the middle style he found in those of Demosthenes. But the examples of illustration followed by detailed analysis are numerous, and it is not possible to do more here than select a few representative criticisms.

In c. 9 there is an admirable analysis of Demosthenes, *Philippic* III, 110, and *Midias* 69. The first of these passages runs as follows: πολλῶν, ὦ ἄνδρες Ἀθηναῖοι, λόγων γινομένων ὀλίγου δεῖν καθ᾽ ἑκάστην ἐκκλησίαν περὶ ὧν Φίλιππος, ἀφ᾽ οὗ τὴν εἰρήνην ἐποιήσατο, οὐ μόνον ὑμᾶς ἀλλὰ καὶ τοὺς ἄλλους ⟨Ἕλληνας⟩ ἀδικεῖ, καὶ πάντων εὖ οἶδ᾽ ὅτι φησάντων γ᾽ ἄν, εἰ καὶ μὴ ποιοῦσι τοῦτο, καὶ λέγειν ⟨δεῖν⟩ καὶ πράττειν, ὅπως ἐκεῖνος παύσεται τῆς ὕβρεως καὶ δίκην δώσει, εἰς τοῦτο ὑπηγμένα πάντα τὰ πράγματα καὶ προειμένα ὁρῶ, ὥστε δέδοικα, μὴ βλάσφημον μὲν εἰπεῖν ἀληθὲς δὲ ᾖ κ.τ.λ. Dionysius first makes a general criticism; the style, he says, is not straightforward and simple, but is contorted and twisted out of the normal and is unnatural. In order to maintain the truth of his assertion, he next

---

[1] Cf. Egger, *op. cit.* p. 137. Egger is misleading, however, when he says "dans la première partie du traité *Sur les anciens orateurs*, nous n'avions eu qu'une comparaison, entre Isée et Lysias"; for Lysias is *contrasted* with Gorgias and Thucydides in *De Lysia* c. 3, and with Isocrates in *De Isocrate* cc. 2–3.

recasts the first part of the passage in a simpler form: πολλῶν, ὦ ἄνδρες Ἀθηναῖοι, λόγων γινομένων καθ᾽ ἑκάστην σχεδὸν ἐκκλησίαν, περὶ ὧν ἀδικεῖ Φίλιππος ὑμᾶς τε καὶ τοὺς ⟨ἄλλους⟩ Ἕλληνας, ἀφ᾽ οὗ τὴν εἰρήνην ἐποιήσατο. He then states his objections in detail; they are (1) the use of ὀλίγου δεῖν for σχεδόν, (2) the wide separation of ἀδικεῖ from its subject Φίλιππος, (3) the unnecessary introduction of οὐ μόνον ὑμᾶς ἀλλὰ καὶ τοὺς ἄλλους Ἕλληνας. Proceeding now to the second half of the quotation Dionysius rewrites: καὶ πάντων λεγόντων, καὶ εἴ τινες τοῦτο μὴ ποιοῦσιν, ὅτι δεῖ καὶ λέγειν καὶ πράττειν ταῦτα, ἐξ ὧν ἐκεῖνος παύσεται τῆς ὕβρεως καὶ δίκην δώσει. His objections are (1) οἶδ᾽ ὅτι is unnecessary, (2) φησάντων γ᾽ ἄν is artificial for φασκόντων. Whatever we may think of the justice of these criticisms, the method employed to express them is beyond reproach. In a second passage (*Philippic* III, 13) Dionysius pursues a similar plan; he recasts the passage in simpler Greek, and then points out that the change of cases and the accumulation of particles renders the original crabbed and artificial. Finally his analysis of the *Midias* passage and his criticism of it on the grounds of the constant incompleteness of its successive clauses is worthy of reproduction; Dionysius' comments, being interspersed in the text of Demosthenes, are translated: " ⟨Ἐμοὶ⟩ δὲ ὃς—this clause is not finished yet—εἴτε τις, ὦ ἄνδρες Ἀθηναῖοι, βούλεται νομίσαι μανίαν—this is a second clause separated from the first and itself incomplete—μανία γὰρ ἴσως ἐστὶν ὑπὲρ δύναμίν τι ποιεῖν—this belongs to neither of the preceding clauses, but is a separate entity—ἢ φιλοτιμίαν—this is a part of the second clause—χορηγὸς ὑπέστην—this completes the opening words."

Further admirable analysis, which can only be briefly sketched here, is to be found in cc. 19 and 20 of the essay, where Dionysius analyses part of the *De Pace* of Isocrates. His chief objections there are to the redundancy of that author, and both his general criticisms and his recasting of diffuse passages in short and compact fashion are excellent. One instance will suffice.[1] Taking the sentence of Isocrates: τίς γὰρ ἂν ἄλλοθεν ἐπελθὼν καὶ μὴ συνδιεφθαρμένος ἡμῖν ἀλλ᾽ ἐξαίφνης ἐπιστὰς τοῖς γιγνομένοις οὐκ ἂν μαίνεσθαι καὶ παραφρονεῖν ἡμᾶς νομίσειεν; οἳ φιλοτιμούμεθα μὲν ἐπὶ τοῖς τῶν προγόνων ἔργοις καὶ τὴν πόλιν ἐκ τῶν τότε πραχθέντων ἐγκωμιάζειν ἀξιοῦμεν, οὐδὲν δὲ τῶν αὐτῶν ἐκείνοις πράττομεν ἀλλὰ πᾶν τοὐναντίον,

[1] I, 167-8.

Dionysius cuts out whole clauses on the ground that they are pure repetition, and rewrites: τίς γὰρ ἂν ἄλλοθεν ἐπελθὼν οὐκ ἂν μαίνεσθαι νομίσειεν ἡμᾶς, οἳ φιλοτιμούμεθα μὲν ἐπὶ τοῖς τῶν προγόνων ἔργοις, οὐδὲν δὲ τῶν αὐτῶν ἐκείνοις πράττομεν; a sentence which makes the point in a much more succinct manner. Succeeding passages are subjected to similar criticism.

Finally, there is considerable analysis and recasting in cc. 24–9, where the *Menexenus* is subjected to a close examination. The standard of the critic's comments there is perhaps slightly lower than in cc. 9–10 and 19–20, and he appears on occasion to be unduly severe; as, for instance, when[1] in the sentence λόγῳ δὲ δὴ τὸν λειπόμενον κόσμον ὅ τε νόμος προστάττει τούτοις ἀποδοῦναι τοῖς ἀνδράσι καὶ χρή he objects to καὶ χρή as redundant; yet it clearly adds a point by stressing moral as opposed to legal obligation.[2] On the other hand he is particularly convincing when he exposes[3] the artificiality of such a sentence as: ἔργων γὰρ εὖ πραχθέντων λόγῳ καλῶς ῥηθέντι μνήμη καὶ κόσμος τοῖς πράξασι γίνεται παρὰ τῶν ἀκουσάντων, or points out the lack of grammatical coherence in such a sentence as that beginning τῆς δ' εὐγενείας πρῶτον ὑπῆρξε τοῖσδε ἡ ⟨τῶν προγόνων⟩ γένεσις in *Men.* 237 b—a sentence which he reproduces in a more straightforward style.[4] As criticism of the style of the *Menexenus* these chapters have considerable merit— provided always that we take into consideration the fact that Dionysius took the *Menexenus* at its face value.

It may be said therefore that in illustration and analysis as well as in comparative criticism this essay far surpasses any previous work. There is also occasionally noticeable in the *De Demosthene* further evidence of the historical point of view in criticism, which was first observed in the *De Isaeo*, and which was noticeable in one passage of the first letter to Ammaeus. The purpose of the essay, as has been already remarked,[5] is to illustrate the preeminence of Demosthenes, not his indebtedness to others; but Dionysius is fully aware of the various influences which helped to shape Demosthenes' style. No

[1] I, 183.
[2] Cf. Meridier, *ad loc.* Hermogenes Π. 'Ιδ. A 228 (= p. 250, Rabe) finds dignity in the sentence.
[3] c. 26 *init.* (= I, 184–5).   [4] c. 27 (= I, 188–9).
[5] See above, p. 27, n. 2.

one predecessor, he now considers, had a radical influence on him; he was, rather, an eclectic, introducing into his style ἐξ ἀπάντων ὅσα κράτιστα καὶ χρησιμώτατα ἦν.[1] This view may seem at first sight to represent a contradiction of the *De Isaeo*; but the development is a natural one. Isaeus was generally considered before Dionysius' time to have had an important influence on Demosthenes, as is clear from the quotation from Pytheas given in *De Isaeo*, c. 4.[2] It was natural therefore for Dionysius to stress this point in his treatment of Isaeus—before he had thoroughly examined the work of Demosthenes. When making a special study of the master orator, Dionysius naturally found other influences too, and in acknowledging them slightly moved his ground.

Having now completed the study of the style of Demosthenes, according to his original plan, Dionysius appears to have become interested in the study of σύνθεσις, and to have produced the *De Comp. Verb.* before returning to Demosthenes. How or when he found this interest it is not possible to say precisely; though the analysis and recasting of passages of Demosthenes such as those examined in *De Dem.* c. 9 border very closely on the subject of σύνθεσις and may conceivably have provided the starting-point for the research which culminated in the *De Compositione Verborum*, a masterpiece of criticism which it now becomes necessary to examine.

It is important to realise that in turning to the *De Compositione Verborum* we are turning to an essay which is not primarily a work of literary criticism in the sense that this term is to be applied to the essays on Lysias, Isocrates, Isaeus, and Demosthenes; instead, we are now dealing with a work of literary theory. Yet there is in the *De Comp. Verb.* considerable comment on the style and practice of individual authors, which, though incidental to the main purpose— that of showing the nature and importance of σύνθεσις—is nevertheless worthy of consideration in the present study. We shall, therefore, not be occupied with the more technical side of the subject of composition, but shall rather judge the merits of passages in which individual authors are criticised, and examine the methods which are employed.

[1] c. 8 (= I, 143), cf. c. 33 (= I, 203).
[2] I, 96 τὸν Ἰσαῖον ὅλον καὶ τὰς τῶν λόγων ἐκείνου τέχνας σεσίτισται (*sc.* ὁ Δημοσθένης).

Although the *De Comp. Verb.* is not so closely concerned with the purpose of μίμησις as are the essays on the orators, it is nevertheless intended primarily as an aid to students of political oratory. Its author announces at the outset that it will be found ἀναγκαιότατον ...ἅπασι...ὁμοίως τοῖς ἀσκοῦσι τοὺς πολιτικοὺς λόγους[1] and shortly afterwards contrasts his work with the treatises of Chrysippus, which he describes as οὐδεμίαν οὔτ' ὠφέλειαν οὔτε χρείαν τοῖς πολιτικοῖς λόγοις συμβαλλομένας.[2] It is not surprising therefore that certain defects in criticism, which are peculiarly the outcome of the rhetorical approach, should be noticeable in the essay. An interesting example occurs near the beginning of the treatise,[3] where Dionysius argues that the arrangement of words is more important, and productive of more charming and striking results than their choice. To prove his contention, he selects two passages, one from Homer, the other from Herodotus. After quoting the former (*Odyssey* XVI, 1–16, on the return of Telemachus) he points out that the fascinating effect of the lines cannot be due to the mere selection of words, since these are so ordinary, so humble, that any farmer, seaman, or artisan might have used them; nor are there to be observed metaphors, hypallages, catachreses, or any other figurative language. "What alternative is there then", says the critic,[4] "but to attribute the beauty of style to the composition?" This is indeed a precarious process of elimination, a typical result of the rhetorical training; Dionysius quite fails to see that the attraction of the passage lies partly in the dramatic beauty of the situation and partly in the very simplicity of the words chosen for the narrative. His comments on the passage of Herodotus (I, 8, the story of Gyges) similarly reveal the singular lack of mental elasticity which was so peculiar a product of the rhetorical training. Here, too, the argument "if it is not ἐκλογή it must be σύνθεσις" is used; other possibilities are excluded, and as has been well observed,[5] all too little allowance is made for "the charming naïveté of Herodotus' mental attitude".

Rhetoric cannot, however, be blamed for certain other flaws which

[1] c. 1 (= II, 3–4). [2] c. 4 (= II, 22).
[3] c. 3 (= II, 9).
[4] II, 11 τί οὖν λείπεται μὴ οὐχὶ τὴν σύνθεσιν τοῦ κάλλους τῆς ἑρμηνείας αἰτιᾶσθαι;
[5] By W. Rhys Roberts, *ad loc.* (p. 84).

mar the essay; for the less convincing criticism is often the outcome of a desire to prove a thesis at all costs. In cc. 17 and 18, for instance, Dionysius argues that "rhythm contributes in no small degree to dignified and impressive composition", and sketches the various "rhythms", or feet, with illustrations, labelling them good or bad. He then proceeds to analyse the opening passage of the *Funeral Oration* of Pericles, the opening sentence of the *Menexenus* (which he had already praised in *De Dem.* c. 24), and the first sentence of the *De Corona*, with the object of showing that only the best "rhythms" are employed. It is very noticeable, however, that the passages might be divided quite differently, and that other "rhythms" might easily be discovered.[1] Dionysius is here too arbitrary, and he himself seems to recognise that other possibilities of division exist. He says, for example, of the sentence ἔργῳ μὲν ἡμῖν οἵδε ἔχουσιν τὰ προσήκοντα σφίσιν αὐτοῖς κ.τ.λ., that the first foot is a bacchius, on the grounds that iambics (which could certainly be discovered in the quotation) are not suited to a funeral oration—a curious example, incidentally, of arguing in a circle![2] So, in the clause ὅσην εὔνοιαν ἔχων ἐγὼ διατελῶ τῇ τε πόλει καὶ πᾶσιν ὑμῖν, Dionysius finds, first a hypobacchius, secondly a bacchius, "*or if you prefer it, a dactyl*";[3] thirdly, a cretic; fourthly, two paeons; fifthly, a molossus or a bacchius, "*for it is possible to scan either way*";[4] and finally, a spondee. Similarly, Dionysius allows himself too much licence in cc. 25 and 26, where he attempts to unmask lines of verse in Demosthenes; the line ἀλλ' εἴπερ ἄρ' ὀρθῶς ἐγὼ λογίζομαι καὶ σκοπῶ is regarded as an iambic trimeter "if the connective ἄρα has its first syllable made long, and further—by your leave—the words καὶ σκοπῶ are regarded as an intermediate excrescence, by means of which the metre is obscured".[5] A remarkable inconsistency also is noticeable in c. 25 where Dionysius

[1] Cf. e.g. Rhys Roberts, p. 178 ("the metrical division seems rather arbitrary") and p. 185 ("it is obvious that we could discover some of these feet in the passage if we were to choose our own way of dividing it").
[2] c. 18 (= II, 76); cf. Rhys Roberts, *ad loc.* (p. 181).
[3] II, 78 εἰ δὲ βούλεταί τις, δάκτυλος.
[4] *Ib.* ἐγχωρεῖ γὰρ ἑκατέρως αὐτὸν διαιρεῖν; cf. Roberts, p. 184, "the *a priori* grounds on which Dionysius...makes his choice between the alternatives which present themselves".
[5] II, 129 (= Roberts, p. 258—I follow Roberts' translation).

argues that the addition of a single syllable would render ὅσην εὔνοιαν ἔχων ἐγὼ διατελῶ an iambic line;[1] yet in c. 18 he had laboriously analysed it into quite different feet! Quite apart from this, Dionysius frequently runs into metrical difficulties in his eagerness to prove his case, and has left more than one editor nonplussed over his apparent disregard of the quantities of the Greek language.[2]

Such are the chief drawbacks of the literary criticism to be found in the *De Comp. Verb.*; but the treatise has also striking merits of exposition, which deserve our careful attention. Chief among these is the power of detailed analysis which is manifested throughout the essay. Hitherto, Dionysius had taken his analysis as far as individual words, as in his criticisms of Isocrates, Thucydides, and Plato; now he goes much beyond this, and considers the effect of syllables, and even of individual letters. He points out[3] that the prolongation of the syllables in Homer's ἠϊόνες βοόωσιν ἐρευγομένης ἁλὸς ἔξω (*Iliad* XVII, 265) is deliberately intended to reproduce the ceaseless reverberation of waves on a windswept shore, while the same device is used to represent the anguish of the Cyclops in Κύκλωψ δὲ στενάχων τε καὶ ὠδίνων ὀδύνῃσιν, χερσὶ ψηλαφόων (*Odyssey* IX, 415–16).[4] Similarly an effect of abruptness is produced "by the docking of syllables and letters" in ἀμβλήδην γοόωσα μετὰ δμωῇσιν ἔειπεν (*Iliad* XXII, 476) and an effect of complete dismay in ἡνίοχοι δ' ἔκπληγεν, ἐπεὶ ἴδον ἀκάματον πῦρ (*Iliad* XVIII, 225).[5] These instances show that Dionysius was now probing much more deeply than hitherto into the secrets of style, and some of his comments show that he had subjected Homer at any rate to a particularly searching examination. So he chooses excellent examples of the "many-voiced" poet's[6] employment of "the finest of the vowels and the softest of the semivowels" in depicting the beauty of youth, such as: καὶ Χλῶριν εἶδον περικαλλέα, τήν ποτε Νηλεὺς γῆμεν ἑὸν μετὰ κάλλος, ἐπεὶ πόρε μυρία ἕδνα (*Odyssey* XI, 281–2), and equally fine examples

---

[1] II, 131 (= Roberts, p. 262).
[2] Cf. Roberts' notes throughout c. 25.
[3] c. 15 (= II, 60; Roberts, p. 154).
[4] *Ib.* (= II, 61; Roberts, p. 156).
[5] *Ib.*
[6] c. 16 (= II, 64; Roberts, p. 160) ὁ δὴ πολυφωνότατος ἁπάντων τῶν ποιητῶν Ὅμηρος.

of the use of strong, resounding syllables to reproduce the rush and
roar of meeting torrents, such as: ὡς δ' ὅτε χείμαρροι ποταμοὶ κατ'
ὄρεσφι ῥέοντες ἐς μισγάγκειαν συμβάλλετον ὄβριμον ὕδωρ (*Iliad* IV,
452–3). But undoubtedly his finest analysis is that in which he makes
a most thorough study[1] of the famous Sisyphus lines in the *Odyssey*
(XI, 593–6):

καὶ μὴν Σίσυφον εἰσεῖδον κρατέρ' ἄλγε' ἔχοντα,
λᾶαν βαστάζοντα πελώριον ἀμφοτέρῃσιν·
ἦ τοι ὁ μὲν σκηριπτόμενος χερσίν τε ποσίν τε
λᾶαν ἄνω ὤθεσκε ποτὶ λόφον.

Dionysius first remarks that the composition brings out the effect
of the weight of the stone, the laborious moving of it, the strain on
the muscles, the push up-hill. He then proceeds to discover the
reason, for he is quite convinced that the effect is not due to chance
or to spontaneous writing. First, he notes the predominance of
monosyllables and dissyllables in the lines in which Sisyphus actually
rolls the stone; then he argues (though he is here more difficult to
follow) that in these lines "the long syllables are half as numerous
again as the short ones"; and, finally, he remarks on the concurrence
of vowels and the juxtaposition of semi-vowels and mutes, as well as
on the use of the longest possible rhythms. The predominance of
monosyllabic and dissyllabic words, he points out, with the resulting
intervals between them, suggest the duration of the action; the long
syllables reproduce the resistance, the heaviness, the difficulty; and
the juxtaposition of rough letters indicates the pauses in Sisyphus'
efforts, the delays, and the vastness of the toil. Then the critic points
out that with the words ἀλλ' ὅτε μέλλοι ἄκρον ὑπερβαλέειν there is a
quickening and bracing effect leading up to τότ' ἐπιστρέψασκε
κραταιΐς· αὖτις ἔπειτα πέδονδε κυλίνδετο λᾶας ἀναιδής. "Have not the
words rolled down", he remarks, "with the weight of the rock, or
rather has not the speed of the narration even outstripped the rush
of the stone?" Again he seeks the explanation; it lies in the predominance of polysyllabic words which hurry the lines on, the
prevalence of short syllables, which drag it forward head-over-heels,
the lack of any appreciable interval between the words which
(caused by clashes of vowels or of semi-vowels) would interfere with

[1] c. 20 (= II, 90; Roberts, p. 202).

the speed of the line, and the employment of the maximum number of dactyls. All this is indeed excellent analysis, which reveals not only a penetrating mind, but a real enthusiasm for literature. It is true that Dionysius may have to face the objection that much of Homer's artistry may have been unconscious, or at any rate subconscious;[1] but as an example of methodical study this passage would be hard to surpass. There is elsewhere in the *De Comp. Verb.* equally detailed, if less convincing, analysis, particularly in the chapters in which Dionysius (still true to the rhetorical instinct) sets forth and illustrates the three types of σύνθεσις (cc. 22–4); but the examples given must suffice as indications of the development which has taken place.

There is, moreover, in the *De Comp. Verb.* a further interesting extension of the use of the method of recasting. In the *De Demosthene* Dionysius had employed this in order to show how an awkwardly written passage should have been written; he now uses it to very good effect in showing how the slightest disturbance of a well-written passage would spoil it and deprive it of its charm or power. He takes, for instance,[2] the sentence of Thucydides (III, 57): ὑμεῖς τε, ὦ Λακεδαιμόνιοι, ἡ μόνη ἐλπίς, δέδιμεν μὴ οὐ βέβαιοι ἦτε, a sentence which he describes as "delightfully arranged, and full of deep feeling", and recasts it as follows: ὑμεῖς τε, ὦ Λακεδαιμόνιοι, δέδιμεν μὴ οὐ βέβαιοι ἦτε, ἡ μόνη ἐλπίς. Clearly, he remarks, the charm and the feeling are gone. Then again, as a further proof, he quotes[3] the sentence of Demosthenes (*De Corona* § 119): τὸ λαβεῖν οὖν τὰ διδόμενα ὁμολογῶν ἔννομον εἶναι, τὸ χάριν τούτων ἀποδοῦναι παρανόμων γράφῃ, and alters the order of words so that it reads: ὁμολογῶν οὖν ἔννομον εἶναι τὸ λαβεῖν τὰ διδόμενα, παρανόμων γράφῃ τὸ τούτων χάριν ἀποδοῦναι. Here too, he points out, the conciseness and effectiveness are lost. One final example, perhaps the best of all, may be adduced. Suppose Demosthenes, he says,[4] had written

---

[1] Cf. Roberts' note on p. 205.

[2] c. 7 (= II, 31; Roberts, pp. 111–12).   [3] *Ib.*

[4] c. 8 (= II, 32; Roberts, p. 114). The passage was a stock example of κλῖμαξ in the rhetorical schools; cf. *Auctor ad Herennium*, IV, 25, 34; Demetrius, Π. Ἑρμ. § 270; Quintilian IX, 3, 55; Hermogenes Π. Ἰδ. A 287 (p. 304, Rabe); Aquila Romanus (Halm, *Rhet. Lat. Min.* p. 34). Cf. also Goodwin's edn. of the *De Corona, ad loc.*

(*De Corona* § 179) ταῦτ' εἰπὼν ἔγραψα, γράψας δ' ἐπρέσβευσα, πρεσβεύσας δ' ἔπεισα Θηβαίους—how much less attractive would this have been than οὐκ εἶπον μὲν ταῦτα, οὐκ ἔγραψα δέ· οὐδ' ἔγραψα μέν, οὐκ ἐπρέσβευσα δέ· οὐδ' ἐπρέσβευσα μέν, οὐκ ἔπεισα δὲ Θηβαίους! Clearly, the method of recasting is used in a novel and most convincing manner.

The latter portion of the *De Demosthene*, which we have next to consider, is hardly more than an appendix in which the principles evolved in *De Comp. Verb.* are re-stated and applied to Demosthenes. As in the latter chapters of the *De Comp. Verb.* Dionysius had been concerned with the three types of σύνθεσις, so in the *De Demosthene*, after a brief summary of the results obtained in cc. 1–33, he proceeds to explain the characteristics of these types, and to argue that Demosthenes is master of them all. It is clear that he is modelling his treatment of Demosthenes' σύνθεσις on the lines he had followed in describing his general χαρακτήρ. His descriptions and illustrations of the αὐστηρά and γλαφυρά ἁρμονία are alike excellent, and it is easy to perceive that Dionysius' prolonged study of composition has rendered him not only a more sensitive critic, but also a closer observer of the minutest details of prose style.

Of particular interest to the student of critical method is the examination of Demosthenes' σύνθεσις conducted in c. 43 of the essay. Dionysius' contention is that Demosthenes uses either the rough or the smooth type of composition to suit his purpose[1]— whether it be to arouse or to soothe his audience—but reveals his consummate art in varying his composition so constantly that the listener fails to perceive that it has any effect. To illustrate his argument Dionysius carefully analyses the composition of a few sentences taken at random from the *Second Olynthiac*. He points out[2] that in the words εἰ δέ τις ὑμῶν, ὦ ἄνδρες Ἀθηναῖοι, τὸν Φίλιππον εὐτυχοῦντα ὁρῶν ταύτῃ φοβερὸν προσπολεμῆσαι νομίζει, σώφρονος μὲν ἀνθρώπου προνοίᾳ χρῆται there is little to disturb the smoothness of flow; two examples of hiatus are to be found in ὦ ἄνδρες and εὐτυχοῦντα ὁρῶν, and two or three examples of the clash of semi-vowels and mutes which do not in the course of nature easily fit

[1] Again the artificiality of conception noticed above (p. 62) is to be observed.
[2] I, 224–6.

together, such as τὸν Φίλιππον and φοβερὸν προσπολεμῆσαι; but apart from these there are few characteristics of the αὐστηρὰ ἁρμονία. In the next sentence, however, μεγάλη γὰρ ῥοπή, μᾶλλον δὲ ὅλον ἡ τύχη παρὰ πάντ' ἐστὶ τὰ τῶν ἀνθρώπων πράγματα, the juxtaposition of γὰρ ῥοπή, ἀνθρώπων πράγματα and δὲ ὅλον is responsible for a somewhat rougher effect. Then the orator returns to a fairly smooth period with οὐ μὴν ἀλλ' ἔγωγε, εἴ τις αἵρεσίν μοι δοίη, τὴν τῆς ἡμετέρας πόλεως τύχην ἂν ἑλοίμην ἐθελόντων, ἃ προσήκει, ποιεῖν ὑμῶν καὶ κατὰ μικρόν, ἢ τὴν ἐκείνου in which ἔγωγε εἶ, αἵρεσίν μοι, and ἡμετέρας πόλεως alone slightly disturb the flow. In fact, the critic declares, in these three sentences, the γλαφυρὰ ἁρμονία definitely predominates. This is, however, far from being so in the next passage, which runs πολὺ γὰρ πλείους ἀφορμὰς εἰς τὸ τὴν παρὰ τῶν θεῶν εὔνοιαν ἔχειν ὁρῶ ὑμῖν ἐνούσας ἢ ἐκείνῳ. ἀλλ', οἴομαι, καθήμεθα οὐδὲν ποιοῦντες· οὐκ ἔνι δ' αὐτὸν ἀργοῦντα οὐδὲ φίλοις ἐπιτάττειν, μή τί γε θεοῖς, where the clashes are frequent and the τραχύτητες numerous. Then again the orator reverts to the smooth, easy-flowing style. It is in this constant variation of ἁρμονίαι, Dionysius concludes, that the supremacy of Demosthenes as a stylist lies, and it is this which entitles him to be said to have perfected a middle type of composition—a type which, we may add, is like the μέσος χαρακτὴρ λέξεως in that it lacks a definite individuality, being formed by a selection of the leading characteristics of the other two types.[1] However, although the process of subdivision is again marked in these chapters, the illustration of the types from Thucydides, Isocrates, and Herodotus and the analysis of passages of Demosthenes already set forth show that in critical exposition Dionysius fully maintains the high standard of the *De Comp. Verb.* In one respect, indeed, he may be considered to have surpassed that standard, for whereas in the special treatise on σύνθεσις he tended to force his texts to prove his contention, in the latter part of the *De Demosthene* he shows a greater readiness to let the text speak for itself.

Of the *Epistula ad Pompeium*, which followed the appearance of the *De Demosthene*, only the first two chapters call for consideration, since the remainder is but an excerpt from the *De Imitatione*. These

[1] Cf. *C.P.* XXXIII (1938), pp. 261-2.

chapters do not contain any further development in critical method, but they do represent a strong defence of the method of comparative criticism adopted in the earlier part of the *De Demosthene*. Dionysius hastens to assure Pompeius at the outset that he, too, is an admirer of Plato's style, but that Plato must submit to comparison with the other great prose writers if any real criterion in prose style is to be found. He carefully points out that he did not set out either to disparage Plato or to write a panegyric of him, but simply to compare him as a stylist with Demosthenes. By no other method could the supremacy of Demosthenes be proved, for "many things which in themselves are thought beautiful and worthy of admiration appear to fall short of their reputation when set side by side with other things that are better".[1] He himself claims that he is far from being the first to realise ὅτι κράτιστος ἐλέγχου τρόπος ὁ κατὰ σύγκρισιν γιγνόμενος. Finally, Dionysius quotes[2] the verdict which he had passed on Plato's style in *De Demosthene* cc. 5–7, and maintains that in reality his view and that of Pompeius are very little apart.

It is noticeable, however, that Dionysius makes no further reference to the chapters which must have caused Pompeius most annoyance—the chapters in which he had examined the *Menexenus*. Pompeius' remark that he could defend much of what Dionysius had attacked, and his complaint that Dionysius had taken exception to a few of these errors which should be graciously conceded to men of genius,[3] find no real answer in the *Epistula ad Pompeium*. But the important point in this letter, for the present purpose, is that it defends a method consciously adopted, which had, despite this one less successful application, been productive of much sound and enlightening criticism.

In conclusion, it may be said that, in these essays of the middle period, Dionysius raised his standard of criticism far beyond that

---

[1] *Ep. ad Pomp.* c. 1 (= II, 223). πολλὰ γὰρ τῶν καθ᾽ αὑτὰ φαινομένων καλῶν καὶ θαυμαστῶν ἑτέροις ἀντιπαρατεθέντα κρείττοσιν ἐλάττω τῆς δόξης ἐφάνη.

[2] c. 2 (= II, 226–30).

[3] Cf. Horace, *A.P.* 347 ff. In *De Thuc.* c. 3 (= I, 328) Dionysius acknowledges this point of view: οὐδεμία γὰρ αὐτάρκης ἀνθρώπου φύσις οὔτ᾽ ἐν λόγοις οὔτ᾽ ἐν ἔργοις ἀναμάρτητος εἶναι, κρατίστη δὲ ἡ πλεῖστα μὲν ἐπιτυγχάνουσα, ἐλάχιστα δὲ ἀστοχοῦσα.

achieved in his earlier studies. He has constantly illustrated his arguments; his analysis is more frequent and more penetrating; his use of the method of recasting has been increased and extended; his comparative criticism has improved beyond measure. His progress is, it would seem, partly due to his enthusiasm for Demosthenes, and partly due to his entry into original research into the problem of style. The rhetorical system is still employed, and there is plenty of evidence of the rhetorical outlook; but there is less mechanical criticism than in the earlier essays, and a marked development in power of expression. The essays of the middle group, it is interesting to notice, are almost entirely concerned with matters of style; we next proceed to the last extensive critical effort of Dionysius, his study of Thucydides, in which subject-matter plays almost as important a part as style.

CHAPTER V

The later essays—on Thucydides, and the second letter to Ammaeus

THE essay on Thucydides, which is next in order of composition, has aroused more interest than any other critical work of Dionysius, with the possible exception of the *De Compositione Verborum.* Many of Dionysius' comments, especially those on Thucydides' treatment of his subject-matter, have provoked dissent among scholars, and even as early as the first century A.D. we find an anonymous author, of whose work only a fragment survives, staunchly defending Thucydides against the criticisms of Dionysius.[1] On the other hand, it is generally admitted that much of what Dionysius has to say about the style of Thucydides is just and well expressed. In the present chapter it will be our aim, not so much to pass an opinion upon the justice or injustice of Dionysius' remarks,[2] as to consider his general outlook upon his subject, and, more particularly, to study the manner in which his criticisms are formulated.

It is clear even from a superficial glance at the *De Thucydide* that the outlook of Dionysius is still that of the rhetorician; the practical purpose of μίμησις, which had tended to slip into the background in the *De Comp. Verb.* and the latter part of the *De Demosthene*, now reappears and takes a prominent place. Thucydides' choice of subject, his avoidance of myth, his strict impartiality win the critic's

---

[1] See *Oxyrhynchus Papyri* VI (1908), no. 853 (commentary of an anonymous author on Thucydides II).

[2] To this question editors of Thucydides and other scholars have given much attention. See also the following special studies: E. Hesse, *D.H. de Thucydide iudicia examinantur* (Leisnig, 1877); J. Wichmann, *D.H. de Thucydide iudicia componuntur et examinantur* (Halis Saxonum, 1878); M. Mille, "Le jugement de Denys d'Halicarnasse sur Thucydide" (*Annales de la Faculté des Lettres de Bordeaux*, 1889, pp. 83–101); G. Pavano, "Dionisio d' Alicarnasso, critico di Tucidide" (*Memorie della R. Accademia delle Scienze di Torino*, LXVIII, 1936).

approval and are characterised as καλά καὶ μιμήσεως ἄξια.¹ Similarly ἄξια ζήλου τε καὶ μιμήσεως are such narratives as that of the last sea-battle in Syracuse harbour (Thuc. VII, 69–72).² Certain of Thucydides' speeches, too, are ζηλωτὰ ἔργα, and suitable as models both for historians and for forensic orators;³ others are to be neither admired nor imitated.⁴ Finally, the critic's aim in studying the style of Thucydides is, in his own words, τὴν ὠφέλειαν αὐτῶν τῶν βουλησομένων μιμεῖσθαι τὸν ἄνδρα.⁵

It is this preoccupation with rhetorical purposes which is responsible for some of the more short-sighted criticisms in the essay. When Dionysius criticises Thucydides for dealing with events in an illogical order (cc. 9–12) or for magnifying trivial incidents and doing scant justice to important ones (cc. 13–20), or for allowing Pericles to upbraid the angry mob instead of appeasing it even to the extent of resorting to tears (cc. 44–5), or for being singularly lacking in propriety in the Melian Dialogue (cc. 37–41), he is not speaking as a true critic, but as a rhetorician whose preconceptions concerning τάξις, αὔξησις, and τὸ πρέπον are the direct result of his special training and vocation. Indeed upon occasion he does not scruple to adopt openly the rules of the rhetorical manuals as his criterion.⁶

There is, however, an explanation for this reversal to the narrower rhetorical point of view, which has not always been given the prominence which it deserves. In the *De Compositione Verborum* and the latter half of the *De Demosthene* Dionysius had been engaged in quiet research, away from issues of immediate practical importance. In the *De Thucydide*, however, he was taking part in a controversy which was clearly being vigorously carried on in the

¹ *De Thuc.* c. 8 *sub fin.* (= I, 335).
² c. 27 *init.* (= I, 371).
³ c. 42 (= I, 398) εἰς τοὺς ἀληθινοὺς ἀγῶνας ἐπιτήδειοι...ἀπὸ τούτων τὰ μιμήματα τοῖς ἱστοριογραφοῦσιν ὑποτίθεμαι λαμβάνειν. Cf. c. 48 (= I, 405) πάθους ἐστὶν ἐναγωνίου μεστά· οἷς ἂν καὶ ἐν δικαστηρίῳ χρήσαιτό τις καὶ ἐν ἐκκλησίαις καὶ φίλοις διαλεγόμενος and c. 49 (= I, 408), and especially Dionysius' curious defence in c. 51 *init.* (= I, 410).
⁴ c. 48 (= I, 406).
⁵ c. 25 (= I, 364).
⁶ c. 19 (= I, 353) οὔτε ὁ τῆς τέχνης ὑπαγορεύει λόγος οὕτω μεθοδεύειν τὰς αὐξήσεις κ.τ.λ.

rhetorical schools, and which appears, indeed, to have created two
or even three marked divisions of opinion within the schools themselves.[1] We are on the battle-ground of the rhetoricians, and the
question over which the strife has arisen is "How far, if at all, is the
student of forensic oratory to make use of the work of the historian
as a model?" Before we consider Dionysius' reply to this question
it will be well to go back a little earlier in the history of the controversy. In the generation before Dionysius, Cicero had dis-
tinguished between the purpose and manner of the historian and the
orator, and in so doing had laid particular stress on the unsuitability
of Thucydides as a model. Those who "profess themselves
followers of Thucydides", who think that when they give vent to
"a few curt and incoherent phrases" they are, each of them, "a down-
right Thucydides", earn but his deepest scorn.[2] But this "novum
quoddam imperitorum et inauditum genus"[3] evidently survived
longer than Cicero perhaps anticipated; for they are the very sect
whose extravagant admiration of Thucydides engendered the
polemic which produced the De Thucydide. Very early in his essay
Dionysius expresses his disapproval of those οἱ κανόνα τῆς ἱστορικῆς
πραγματείας ἐκεῖνον ὑποτίθενται τὸν ἄνδρα (sc. τὸν Θουκυδίδην) καὶ
τῆς περὶ τοὺς πολιτικοὺς λόγους δεινότητος ὅρον.[4] In the middle of
his essay[5] he has a longer and more scathing indictment, in the course
of which (in a simile which recalls Lucretius)[6] he ridicules the
devotion of those who see every virtue in their beloved author, and
strongly resent any attempt to remove him from his pedestal.
Finally, in his concluding chapter,[7] Dionysius refuses to join either
those who have nothing but praise for Thucydides, or those who
find no place for him whatever within the rhetorical scheme; instead,
he takes a middle view, based upon the results of his own investigation.

[1] This I gather from Dionysius' closing remarks in c. 55 (= 1, 418).
[2] Orator, § 32 "sed cum mutila quaedam et hiantia locuti sunt, quae vel
sine magistro facere potuerunt, germanos se putant esse Thucydidas".
Cf. Brutus, § 287.
[3] Ib. § 30.   [4] c. 2 (= 1, 327).
[5] c. 35 (= 1, 381).
[6] IV, 1141–62; cf. Egger, op. cit. p. 223.
[7] c. 55 (= 1, 417–18).

Contemporary controversy, therefore, is responsible for the unusually strong emphasis laid on the principle of μίμησις in this essay. However, quite apart from the general rhetorical outlook, the method of criticism adopted in the *De Thucydide* is also largely influenced by the rhetorical system. The essay falls into two clearly defined sections, that on the πραγματικὸς τόπος (cc. 5–20), and that on the λεκτικὸς τόπος (cc. 21–55). Moreover, in each of these main divisions we encounter subdivisions. The πραγματικὸς τόπος is resolved into chapters on ὑπόθεσις (cc. 6–8), διαίρεσις (c. 9), τάξις (cc. 10–12), and ἐξεργασίαι (cc. 13–20).[1] The scheme of the λεκτικὸς τόπος is fully set forth (c. 22) with its tripartite division into ἐκλογή, σύνθεσις, and σχήματα, and the subdivisions of the first into κυρία and τροπικὴ φράσις, the second into κόμματα, κῶλα, and περίοδοι, and the third into σχήματα ἁπλῶν ὀνομάτων and σχήματα συνθέτων ὀνομάτων; finally the ἀρεταί are mentioned, with their division into ἀναγκαῖαι and ἐπίθετοι. In the chapters which immediately follow this précis of the λεκτικὸς τόπος (cc. 23–4), considerable use of it is made for purposes of criticism, for the styles of the early λογογράφοι, Herodotus, and Thucydides are each treated according to their ἐκλογή, σύνθεσις, and σχήματα, while there is also one example of the reappearance of the ἀναγκαῖαι and ἐπίθετοι ἀρεταί. It is, however, interesting to notice that after this point (c. 25 onwards) there is comparatively little evidence of actual criticism according to stock divisions[2] in the remaining thirty chapters, which are devoted to a thorough examination of the style of Thucydides. To the merits of exposition, then, of the whole essay, and these chapters in particular, we may now turn.

It is in the extent of its illustration and analysis that the *De Thucydide* surpasses the essays of both the early and the middle periods. Whatever adverse criticism some (though by no means all) of Dionysius' comments may have aroused, there can be little doubt that he has set forth, explained, and illustrated his views in a manner that leaves little to be desired. The essay on Thucydides, together with its supplement, the second letter to Ammaeus, offers

[1] Cf. the subdivisions used in the excerpt from the Περὶ Μιμήσεως (*Ep. ad Pomp.* c. 3). See above, p. 40.

[2] Traces are seen in c. 26 *init.* (= I, 366), c. 42 (= I, 397), and c. 48 (= I, 405).

us far more criticism of a single author than any previous study, and those merits of exposition, the gradual growth of which we have traced, are here seen at their best.

Illustration and analysis in the *De Thucydide* are not confined to the treatment of the λεκτικὸς τόπος but are also found in that of the πραγματικὸς τόπος, to which, as it is dealt with first in the essay, we may first turn. After contrasting Thucydides with his predecessors, and praising him for his choice of subject[1] and painstaking search for truth (cc. 5–8),[2] Dionysius complains that by dividing his narrative according to summers and winters (διαίρεσις), Thucydides loses clarity and makes it difficult for his readers to follow the course of events (c. 9).[3] To prove his point, he analyses the third book of Thucydides. First, he observes, Thucydides begins the narrative of the revolt of Mitylene (i.e. cc. 2–14), but, before completing his account, turns to the activities of the Spartans (cc. 15 ff.), and then, without putting the final touch to these, takes up the narrative of the siege of Plataea (cc. 20 ff.); however, leaving this also unfinished, he returns to Mitylene (cc. 35 ff.). Next he gives his account of the στάσις at Corcyra (cc. 70 ff.) but, again, leaving it half-finished, introduces a short account of the first Athenian expedition to Sicily (cc. 86, 88, 90). We then have the expedition of the Athenians to the Peloponnese (c. 91), and that of the Spartans against the Dorians (c. 92), the exploits of Demosthenes at Leucas, and the war with the Aetolians (cc. 94 ff.). After this the historian goes off to Naupactus (c. 102), but, leaving the mainland wars unfinished, returns to Sicily (c. 103), and then proceeds to recount the purification of Delos (c. 104), the attack of the Ambraciots upon Amphilochian Argos (cc. 105 ff.), and so on. In short, "the whole book is chopped up in this manner, and continuity of narrative is lost".[4] It has been well observed[5] that Dionysius exaggerates the lack of

---

[1] Contrast his former verdict in Περὶ Μιμήσεως (*Ep. ad Pomp.* c. 3 = II, 233–4).

[2] Here also Dionysius is more fair to Thucydides than in *Ep. ad Pomp. loc. cit.* (= II, 238).

[3] Cf. II, 237.

[4] I, 337 ὅλη γὰρ ἡ βύβλος οὕτω συγκέκοπται καὶ τὸ διηνεκὲς τῆς ἀπαγγελίας ἀπολώλεκε.

[5] By Egger, *op. cit.* p. 192.

connection between events in order to prove his thesis; but the student of critical method must give him credit for so fully expounding his point.

Next (cc. 10 ff.), Dionysius takes sides with those critics who object to the order (τάξις) in which events are described by Thucydides, particularly in his first book, which he proceeds to analyse in order to make his argument clear. Thucydides, he points out, begins with a general preface on the magnitude and importance of the war, and then proceeds to discuss the causes. These are (i) the ostensible cause, viz. the Athenian expedition sent to the assistance of Corcyra, and (ii) the real cause, viz. Spartan fear of the growth of Athenian power. Thucydides first gives the story of Epidamnus, Corcyra, Potidaea, and the Peloponnesian congress (cc. 24–87), then illustrates the growth of Athenian power, describing it "briefly and superficially" (cc. 89–117), and finally returns to events at Corcyra (cc. 118 ff.). What he should have done, in Dionysius' opinion, was to explain the real cause first, and then to recount the opening incidents which constituted merely the ostensible cause for war.[1] Here again Dionysius, who seems to have had little sympathy for the principle of ὕστερον πρότερον Ὁμηρικῶς, reveals the mental rigidity of the rhetorician in his argument, but has nevertheless fully set forth the evidence upon which he bases his criticism.

Finally (cc. 13 ff.), to conclude his treatment of the πραγματικὸς τόπος, Dionysius criticises Thucydides for excessive or deficient elaboration (ἐξεργασίαι) of the events he describes. Descriptions of sea-battles are sometimes treated at undue length, as for instance at the end of Book II; at other times important engagements are cursorily dismissed, as in I, 100, which is quoted in illustration. Land-battles, too, are sometimes given undue prominence—the affair of Pylos and Sphacteria, for instance, is treated at excessive length, whereas the surrender of the people of Cythera and the capture of the Aeginetans in Thyrea are all too briefly described (IV, 54 and 57, which are also quoted). Similarly, two occasions for the seeking of peace which arose are treated by Thucydides in a very different fashion; the appeal to Sparta after the second invasion of Attica is described "in a careless, half-hearted fashion" (II, 59, quoted), whereas the speech of the Spartan ambassadors sent to

[1] Cf. II, 235.

recover the prisoners taken at Pylos is fully reported (IV, 15–22). The capture and destruction of cities and the enslavement of their inhabitants, though frequently described with great vividness and power, as in the case of Plataea, Mitylene, and Melos, are frequently too superficially treated, as in the case of Scione, Hestiaea, and Aegina (V, 32; I, 114; II, 27, quoted). Speeches, too, are sometimes wrongly omitted, or included at an unsatisfactory point; so the debate of the first day concerning the fate of the Mitylenaeans is entirely omitted, whereas that of the second day, when the μετάνοια took place, is fully described. Even the celebrated Funeral Oration itself is not immune from criticism; Dionysius would rather see it in any book but the second. Thucydides himself, he argues, admits that the number of the fallen was small (II, 22, quoted by Dionysius), and the ἐπιτάφιος could much more fittingly have been pronounced over those who fell with Demosthenes at Pylos, or with Nicias and Demosthenes in the disastrous Sicilian expedition, for to them no such public honour is paid. Finally, Dionysius renews his attack upon the proem, which is "a history all by itself",[1] and packed, in his opinion, with unnecessary discussions, as, for instance, on the name of Ἑλλάς being later than the Trojan War (c. 3), on the early expeditions in search of food (c. 5), on early Athenian luxury as opposed to Spartan frugality and strict discipline (c. 6), on Ameinocles the shipbuilder (c. 13), on Polycrates of Samos (ib.), and on the sea-battle between the Phocians of Massilia and the Carthaginians (ib.). So dissatisfied, in fact, is Dionysius with the proem that he rewrites it in a few pages, omitting cc. 2–20 altogether! It would not be difficult to defend Thucydides against this and other charges made by the critic, which result either from a mistaken application of rhetorical rules, or from a lack of knowledge of the relative importance of events in the Peloponnesian War and the diplomatic and strategic significance of incidents apparently trivial in themselves. But it should be added that Dionysius' treatment of this part of the subject is again marked by thorough illustration and analysis.

To realise the development in power of exposition which has taken place, one has only to turn back to those sections of the *De Lysia* (c. 15) and the *De Isaeo* (cc. 14 ff.) which deal with the

[1] c. 19 (= I, 353) ἱστορία τις αὐτὴ καθ᾽ αὑτήν.

πραγματικὸς τόπος. In the former we have, similarly, criticism of the τάξις and the ἐξεργασίαι of Lysias, but no sort of explanation or illustration whatsoever; in fact, both there and in the *De Isaeo* we have little more than a collection of rhetorical jargon. The discussion of the πραγματικὸς τόπος in the *De Thucydide*, a formidable task which demanded some little courage and independence, is, from the point of exposition at any rate, a far higher achievement.

We may now turn to examine the merits of Dionysius' treatment of the λεκτικὸς τόπος. His first few chapters, as has been observed,[1] are modelled on rhetorical lines, but his examination of the style of Thucydides, which opens at c. 25, is conducted with great thoroughness and detail. From the beginning he declares that he intends to give the reasons why he considers passages well or badly written (παρατιθεὶς . . . τὰς αἰτίας, δι' ἃς τοιαῦτά ἐστι)—an intention which, in general, he fulfils. As his study is divided into criticism of the narratives (cc. 25–33) and of the speeches (cc. 34–49) of Thucydides, it will be well to adopt this order in our own investigation.

Dionysius first gives examples of narrative passages which win his approval from the opening chapter of Book I, from Book IV, c. 34, and from Book VII, cc. 69–72. His comment on the first passage is unfortunately lost owing to a lacuna in the MSS., and on the last he makes no comment, save to give it his enthusiastic approval. But the second passage is re-arranged and rewritten by the critic in the manner which he had adopted with gradually increasing frequency in the earlier essays. His recasting of this passage is rather too long to quote, but its effect is to render the passage less tortuous and more easily read by an alteration of the order of its component clauses. Beyond this, however, Dionysius has no further objection to the passage; it is not until a few chapters further on that he begins his attack on narrative passages which suffer from Thucydides' besetting sin of obscurity (cc. 29 ff.).

The chapter which Dionysius selects for censure is that which contains the celebrated description of στάσις at Corcyra (III, 82). Throughout his examination of this narrative Dionysius not only states his general and particular objections to each sentence, but again and again recasts the original in order to bring home to the reader exactly what it is to which he objects. In four chapters here (cc. 29–

[1] Above, p. 84.

32) he has as many examples of this method of exposition as in all the previous essays taken together. Beginning with the third section of the chapter, he declares that ἐστασίαζέ τε οὖν τὰ τῶν πόλεων is an unnecessary periphrasis for ἐστασίαζον αἱ πόλεις, which would have been a "healthier" way of saying the same thing. Similarly καὶ τὰ ἐφυστερίζοντά που is difficult, and would have been more clearly expressed as αἱ δ᾽ ὑστεροῦσαι πόλεις. The succeeding clause ἐπιπύστει τῶν προγενομένων πολὺ ἐπέφερε τὴν ὑπερβολὴν τοῦ καινοῦσθαι τὰς διανοίας is intended to mean (οἱ δὲ ὑστερίζοντες) ἐπιπυνθανόμενοι τὰ γεγενημένα παρ᾽ ἑτέροις ἐλάμβανον ὑπερβολὴν ἐπὶ τὸ διανοεῖσθαί τι καινότερον. Similarly in the closing phrase τῶν τ᾽ ἐπιχειρήσεων ἐπιτεχνήσει καὶ τῶν τιμωριῶν ἀτοπίᾳ and the following sentence καὶ τὴν εἰωθυῖαν τῶν ὀνομάτων ἀξίωσιν ἐς τὰ ἔργα ἀντήλλαξαν τῇ δικαιώσει, the expressions ἐπιτέχνησις, τῶν τιμωριῶν ἀτοπία, εἰωθυῖα τῶν ὀνομάτων ἀξίωσις, and ἐς τὰ ἔργα ἀντηλλαγμένη δικαίωσις savour of poetical periphrasis, and the sense of this entangled passage is seen if we rewrite πολλὴν τὴν ἐπίδοσιν ἐλάμβανον εἰς τὸ διανοεῖσθαί τι καινότερον περὶ τὰς τέχνας τῶν ἐγχειρημάτων καὶ περὶ τὰς ὑπερβολὰς τῶν τιμωριῶν· τά τε εἰωθότα ὀνόματα ἐπὶ τοῖς πράγμασι λέγεσθαι μετατιθέντες ἄλλως ἠξίουν αὐτὰ καλεῖν. Proceeding to the next sentence Dionysius objects to the paromoioses, parisoses, and epithets introduced for the sake of embellishment, and would rewrite τὴν μὲν γὰρ τόλμαν ἀνδρίαν ἐκάλουν, τὴν δὲ μέλλησιν δειλίαν· οἱ δὲ σώφρονες ἄνανδροι, καὶ οἱ συνετοὶ πρὸς ἅπαντα ἐν ἅπασιν ἀργοί. Further examples of "harsh utterance" (σκληραγωγῶν τὴν λέξιν) follow in the sentence ἀσφάλεια...ὕποπτος, in which it is not clear who is supposed to be angry and for what reason, or who it is that gainsays and on what grounds. As for ἐπιβουλεύσας δέ τις τυχών τε ξυνετός, καὶ ὑπονοήσας ἔτι δεινότερος, the addition of τυχών does not make the meaning any clearer, and τυχών and ὑπονοήσας cannot refer to the same person, since τυχών is used of one who succeeds and attains his object, while ὑπονοήσας refers to one who anticipates a blow that is imminent, but not yet struck. The sense becomes as clear as daylight if the sentence is rewritten οἵ τ᾽ ἐπιβουλεύοντες ἑτέροις εἰ κατορθώσειαν, δεινοί· καὶ οἱ τὰς ἐπιβουλὰς προϋπονοοῦντες εἰ φυλάξαιντο, ἔτι δεινότεροι and continued ὁ δὲ προϊδόμενος, ὅπως μηδὲν αὐτῷ δεήσει μήτ᾽ ἐπιβουλῆς μήτε φυλακῆς, τάς τε ἑταιρίας διαλύειν ἐδόκει καὶ τοὺς

ἐναντίους ἐκπεπλῆχθαι. So the examination proceeds until §§ 3–7 of the chapter are almost entirely rewritten. By recasting Thucydides in this way Dionysius succeeds in removing most of the obscurity, but he also removes the pungency and compactness which he elsewhere[1] acknowledges as characteristic of Thucydides' style; his procedure is rather like attempting to rewrite Tacitus in the style of Caesar or Nepos. However, from the point of view of critical exposition, these chapters provide more sustained analysis than any similar chapters in previous essays.

Turning now to the speeches of Thucydides, which he divides into dialogues (cc. 36–41) and harangues (cc. 42–49), Dionysius adopts the same procedure as in his treatment of the narratives, that is, he first selects speeches that win his approval and then examines those which he considers deserving of censure. As his example of a really satisfactory διάλογος he takes that between the Plataeans and the Spartan army under Archidamus, which was about to ravage their territory. Beyond quoting the relevant chapters (II, 71–4), however, and praising the dialogue as extremely well written, Dionysius does not make any further remark, but hastens to contrast with it the celebrated Melian Dialogue, "which is praised most of all by admirers of the Thucydidean type of style" (c. 37 *init.*).

Dionysius' main objections to the Melian Dialogue are made on the ground of propriety. He occasionally finds fault with the style also, but is chiefly annoyed by what he considers to be the extremely unsuitable tones in which the Athenians press their advantage. A number of chapters are cited to prove this point, and it will perhaps be of interest to give a selection of Dionysius' comments. He objects to the opening of v, 89 on the grounds that "the thought is unworthy of the Athenian people, and inappropriate in such a situation; it is an admission that the expedition is against people who have done nothing wrong".[2] The continuation he finds equally objectionable, for it is equivalent to saying to the Melians "You are right in supposing yourselves the victims of injustice, but accept your inevitable fate and yield; we are quite aware that we are ill-treating you, but we shall overcome your weakness by force."[3]

---

[1] c. 24 (= I, 363) χρώματα δὲ αὐτῆς τό τε στριφνόν, καὶ τὸ πυκνόν κ.τ.λ.

[2] c. 37 (= I, 390).   [3] *Ib.* (= I, 391).

Of the final section of the chapter he says "This would be appropriate for barbarian kings to address to Greeks, but not for the Athenians to address to their fellow-countrymen whom they freed from the Medes." Again, of a sentence in v, 91, "these are words which even pirates and brigands would hardly have used".[1] It is clear that Dionysius quite fails to grasp the dramatic significance of the dialogue, and there is accordingly little value in his comments. However, his occasional remarks on points of style are more noteworthy, and are set forth in the thorough manner already extensively employed. So he finds fault with the sentence ἡ μὲν ἐπιείκεια τοῦ διδάσκειν καθ' ἡσυχίαν ἀλλήλους οὐ ψέγεται· τὰ δὲ τοῦ πολέμου παρόντα ἤδη καὶ οὐ μέλλοντα διαφέροντα αὐτοῦ φαίνετε (v, 86) on the ground that αὐτοῦ does not agree either with the singular ἐπιείκεια or the plural τὰ τοῦ πολέμου, but destroys the natural sequence. Having thus analysed the sentence and stated his objections, Dionysius rewrites, substituting αὐτῆς for αὐτοῦ.[2] Similarly he finds the style of the sentence οὐ γὰρ τοσοῦτον ἡμᾶς βλάπτει ἡ ἔχθρα ὑμῶν ὅσον ἡ φιλία μὲν ἀσθενείας, τὸ δὲ μῖσος δυνάμεως παράδειγμα τοῖς ἀρχομένοις δηλούμενον (v, 95) contorted, and brings out the sense more clearly by rewriting φιλοῦντες μὲν ἡμᾶς ἀσθενεῖς φαίνεσθαι πρὸς τοὺς ἄλλους ποιήσετε, μισοῦντες δὲ ἰσχυρούς· οὐ γὰρ ζητοῦμεν εὐνοίᾳ τῶν ὑπηκόων ἄρχειν, ἀλλὰ φόβῳ.[3] In short, Dionysius shows further evidence here of the methods of analysis and recasting which he employed to the full in dealing with the chapter on στάσις.

Of the harangues of Thucydides,[4] some win high praise from Dionysius on grounds of style and content, such as that of Pericles delivered on the eve of the war (I, 140–4), those of Nicias in favour of the Sicilian Expedition (VI, 9–14 and 20–3), the letter of Nicias from Sicily (VII, 11–15), his address to his troops before the final sea-battle (VII, 61–4), his exhortation to his soldiers before the retreat (VII, 77), and most of all the defence of the Plataeans (III, 53–9). Others obtain only partial approval, such as that in which Pericles defends himself against the people (II, 60–4), those of Cleon and Diodotus concerning the fate of Mitylene (III, 37–40 and

---

[1] c. 39 (= I, 392).   [2] c. 37 (= I, 389).
[3] c. 39 (= I, 392).   [4] cc. 42 ff. (= I, 397).

42–8), that of Hermocrates to the people of Camarina (VI, 76–80), and the reply of Euphemus (VI, 82–7). Of these he proceeds to examine two in some detail, that of Pericles in II, 60–4, and that of Hermocrates in VI, 76–80. In dealing with the former, as with the Melian Dialogue, Dionysius bases his criticisms partly on grounds of propriety, and partly on grounds of style. His criticisms on grounds of propriety are not in the least convincing; he selects passages in which Pericles strongly defends his policy and personal character, and declares them inappropriate in tone, his argument being that Thucydides should, in view of the dangerous situation, have represented Pericles as appealing to the mob, soothing its anger, and gradually preparing the way for his self-justification, and not as reprimanding indignant citizens in so outspoken a manner. It is clear that we have here yet another instance of adhesion to certain fixed rules which Dionysius held appropriate to a given set of circumstances.[1] When, however, he approaches the question of the style of Pericles' speech, and that of Hermocrates, he again fully illustrates his point of view. Those passages of which he approves are set forth in full; those which he finds in any way objectionable are analysed, and the reasons underlying his objection, whether it be obscurity, poetical expression, or frigidity resulting from Gorgianic figures, are in each instance set forth.[2]

In short, we have in the λεκτικὸς τόπος of the *De Thucydide* a more extensive and more thoroughly conducted investigation into an author's style than in any previous essay, the *De Demosthene* not excepted. The *De Thucydide* must have demanded from Dionysius considerably more mental effort than the *De Demosthene*, not only because of the greater difficulty of the task, but also because of the detailed analysis which he made of Thucydides' work; it was much easier for him to select passages from Demosthenes and make a general, and occasionally even detailed, comparison of them with passages from Lysias, Thucydides, and Isocrates than to analyse the style of Thucydides in the various branches of the *History*, and illustrate or defend his point of view at every turn. It has already been observed that the method of recasting an author's remark in

---

[1] Cf. c. 44 (= I, 399) σχῆμά τε οὐ τοῦτο τῇ διανοίᾳ πρεπωδέστατον ἦν, τὸ ἐπιτιμητικόν, ἀλλὰ τὸ παραιτητικόν.

[2] cc. 46–8.

order to bring home a criticism is among the most satisfactory methods of critical exposition, and one which calls for most exertion on the part of the critic. This method is used once in the *De Isocrate*, twice in the *De Isaeo*, nine times in the *De Demosthene*, and some seventeen or eighteen times in the *De Thucydide*. This alone is sufficient indication of the depth and thoroughness of exposition to be found in this essay.

It is also interesting to notice that other merits of earlier essays reappear in the *De Thucydide*. Thucydides is treated not only as an individual writer, but also in relation to other writers of Greek prose—that is to say, there is again noticeable the historical method of approach, and a certain amount of comparative criticism. Before Dionysius makes any criticism of Thucydides, in either the πραγμα-τικὸς or the λεκτικὸς τόπος, he examines the subject-matter and style of earlier historians.[1] In the province of subject-matter the early historians, such as Eugeon, Deiochus, Eudemus, Democles, Hecataeus, Acusilaus, Charon, Melesagoras, Hellanicus, Damastes, Xenomedes, and Xanthus were extremely limited in scope, confining themselves to the history of separate cities and nations. The one exception, Herodotus, planned a far vaster subject, which dealt with 220 years of European and Asiatic history. Thucydides followed neither the early λογογράφοι nor Herodotus, regarding the subjects of the former as too trivial, and the subject of the latter as too extensive to be grasped by the mind at once. Moreover Thucydides made a great advance by entirely dispensing with the mythological element which detracted from the historical value of so many of his predecessors, and followed only the most trust-worthy authorities, where he lacked personal knowledge of the facts. Finally, Thucydides is strictly impartial; he neither adds to, nor detracts from, the truth; he is free from any suspicion of jealousy or flattery, and he does justice to the characters, however diverse, who appear in his work. In style also[2] Thucydides differs from his predecessors, and also from his contemporaries; for whereas they almost to a man adopted a plain, unadorned style, the charm of which lay in its simplicity and which gave them (Herodotus again excepted) no scope for brilliance or sustained power, Thucydides deliberately adopted a style that was figurative,

[1] cc. 5 ff.   [2] cc. 23 ff.

pungent, full of vigour, brief to the point of obscurity, the aim of which appeared to be to crush as much thought as possible into the fewest words.

Nor is Thucydides compared and contrasted only with contemporaries and predecessors; in the last three chapters of the essay (cc. 53–5), his influence on Demosthenes is mentioned and illustrated by several passages of the orator's work. Dionysius' conclusion is the same as in the *De Demosthene* (c. 10); he finds a great similarity in the avoidance by both of the natural, straightforward manner of expression, but a difference in the frequent tendency of Thucydides to obscurity, as contrasted with the intelligibility of Demosthenes, even though his expression be involved.

Dionysius no doubt thought that, having fulfilled his promise to compose a special treatise on Thucydides, he would be free to return to his interrupted labours on the orators. But such was not to be the case; for his friend Ammaeus, upon receiving a copy of this latest treatise, pressed for further elucidation and illustration of some of the remarks therein contained. Dionysius' reply betrays some impatience at this further request, and it may well be supposed that he did not find the task of making an even more detailed investigation into Thucydides' style a particularly agreeable one.[1] However, his short letter of seventeen brief chapters is full of material, and by its wealth of illustration makes a valuable appendix to the *De Thucydide*.

In the *De Thucydide* (c. 24), Dionysius had briefly indicated that Thucydides' style was characterized by its obscure, archaic, and puzzling expressions, and its remarkable variety and novelty in constructions; these latter he fully enumerates, but does not explain by illustration, and it is this section of the *De Thucydide* which Ammaeus now requires to be further elucidated. Dionysius, in accordance with Ammaeus' suggestion, briefly gives the evidence on which his several remarks are based. We have, as a result, in the second letter to Ammaeus, no less than thirty passages of Thucydides quoted in illustration, of which several are analysed and a few subjected to the process of recasting so frequently employed in the larger work. A brief summary will indicate the extent of this

[1] *Ep. ad Ammaeum II init.* (= 1, 321), cf. Egger, *op. cit.* p. 233.

illustration. First (c. 3) five examples are given of "obscure, archaic, and puzzling" expressions, viz. ἀκραιφνής (ι, 19, 52), ὁ ἐπιλογισμός, ἡ περιωπή (ιν, 86), and ἡ ἀνακωχή (ι, 40, 66, III, 4, IV, 38, 117, V, 25, 26, 32, VIII, 87); they are followed by four examples of "poetical" expressions, viz. ἡ κωλύμη (ι, 92, ιν, 27, 63), ἡ καταβοή (ι, 73, VIII, 85, 87), ἡ ἀχθηδών (II, 37, ιν, 40), and ἡ δικαίωσις (ι, 141, III, 82, IV, 86, V, 17, VIII, 66). Next (c. 4), examples are given of periphrasis, as I, 138 ἦν γὰρ ὁ Θεμιστοκλῆς βεβαιότατα δὴ φύσεως Ισχὺν δηλώσας καὶ διαφερόντως τι ἐς αὐτὸ μᾶλλον ἑτέρου ἄξιος θαυμάσαι (where presumably Dionysius objects to ἦν δηλώσας for ἐδεδηλώκει, and to μᾶλλον ἑτέρου as redundant after διαφερόντως τι), and II, 37; to illustrate the opposite fault of brachylogy, the use of παρεξειρεσία in IV, 12 is cited, and expanded to τὰ προέχοντα μέρη τῆς εἰρεσίας. In the following chapters (5, 6) Thucydides' use of nouns in place of verbs, and of verbs in place of nouns, is illustrated, the former from ι, 41 δικαιώματα μὲν οὖν τάδε πρὸς ὑμᾶς ἔχομεν, παραίνεσιν δὲ καὶ ἀξίωσιν χάριτος τοιάνδε and I, 143, the latter from I, 23 τὴν μὲν οὖν ἀληθεστάτην αἰτίαν, λόγῳ δὲ ἀφανεστάτην, τοὺς Ἀθηναίους οἶομαι μεγάλους γινομένους ἀναγκάσαι εἰς τὸ πολεμεῖν (where Dionysius would have written μεγάλοι γιγνόμενοι οἱ Ἀθηναῖοι ἀνάγκην παρέσχον τοῦ πολέμου). Next (cc. 7-8), we are given examples of the use of active for passive, such as I, 144 οὔτε γὰρ ἐκεῖνο κωλύει ταῖς σπονδαῖς οὔτε τόδε (where Dionysius would require κωλύεται), and ι, 2 τῆς γὰρ ἐμπορίας οὐκ οὔσης, οὐδ' ἐπιμιγνύντες ἀδεῶς ἀλλήλοις (where Dionysius would write ἐπιμιγνύμενοι), and the converse, as in I, 120, ἡμῶν δὲ ὅσοι μὲν Ἀθηναίοις ἤδη ἐνηλλάγησαν (where συνήλλαξαν is required), and ib. τοὺς δ' ἐν τῇ μεσογείᾳ μᾶλλον κατῳκημένους (where Dionysius would write κατῳκηκότας). Thucydides' use of singular for plural and plural for singular is next illustrated (c. 9), the former from VI, 78 καὶ εἴ τῳ ἄρα παρέστηκεν τὸν μὲν Συρακόσιον, αὐτὸν δὲ οὐ πολέμιον εἶναι τῷ Ἀθηναίῳ (where Dionysius, rather quibblingly, requires the plural), and IV, 10 (τὸν πολέμιον for τοὺς πολεμίους), and the latter from II, 35, where the singular ἕκαστος is followed by the plural. Interchange of genders is the next peculiarity of Thucydides which Dionysius illustrates (c. 10); he selects four examples, τάραχος for ταραχή, ὄχλος for ὄχλησις (ι, 73), τὸ βουλόμενον for ἡ βούλησις (ι, 90, VII, 49) and τὸ δυνάμενον for ἡ δύναμις (II, 97?),

96   DIONYSIUS OF HALICARNASSUS

and quotes two passages in illustration, VI, 24 οἱ δὲ Ἀθηναῖοι τὸ μὲν βουλόμενον οὐκ ἀφηρέθησαν ὑπὸ τοῦ ὀχλώδους τῆς παρασκευῆς, and IV, 78 ὥστε εἰ μὴ τῇ δυναστείᾳ μᾶλλον ἢ ἰσονομίᾳ ἐχρῶντο τῷ ἐπιχωρίῳ οἱ Θεσσαλοί. So the study proceeds; Thucydides' use of cases (c. 11) and tenses (c. 12), his constructions according to the sense (c. 13), his employment of persons for things and things for persons (c. 14), his awkward parentheses (c. 15), his involved and tortuous construction (c. 16), and his affected figures (c. 17) are all carefully illustrated from the text.

As examples of the method of recasting, which is also a noticeable feature of the essay, two passages of c. 11 may be taken. Speaking of Thucydides' abnormal case-usage, Dionysius cites VIII, 64: σωφρο-σύνην γὰρ λαβοῦσαι αἱ πόλεις καὶ ἄδειαν τῶν πρασσομένων ἐχώρησαν ἐπὶ τὴν ἄντικρυς ἐλευθερίαν, τῆς ἀπὸ τῶν Ἀθηναίων ὑπούλου εὐνομίας οὐ προτιμήσαντες, and points out that writers whose syntax conformed to normal usage would not only have retained the feminine form of the participle, but would also have written an accusative instead of a genitive case, as follows: σωφροσύνην γὰρ λαβοῦσαι αἱ πόλεις καὶ ἄδειαν τῶν πρασσομένων ἐχώρησαν ἐπὶ τὴν ἄντικρυς ἐλευθερίαν τὴν ἀπὸ τῶν Ἀθηναίων ὕπουλον εὐνομίαν οὐ προτιμήσασαι. Similarly, in IV, 10, Thucydides writes καὶ μὴ τῷ πλήθει αὐτῶν καταπλαγέντες, whereas in Dionysius' opinion he should have written καὶ μὴ τὸ πλῆθος τῶν πολεμίων καταπλαγέντες just as one would be said, not τῇ παρὰ τῶν θεῶν ὀργῇ φοβεῖσθαι, but τὴν τῶν θεῶν ὀργήν.

The second letter to Ammaeus, however, although it is in itself a thorough exposition, is not to be regarded as a separate work of criticism. It is intended by Dionysius as an appendix, to be taken in close conjunction with the larger work. In order therefore to gain a true estimate of the critic's exposition in his latest period, we must consider the De Thucydide mainly, using the letter to Ammaeus only as supplementary evidence.

If the critic's work on Thucydides be now compared with the essays of the early and middle periods,[1] it is first of all clear that the practical purpose of μίμησις still dominates the work as it did in the beginning; in this essay in particular, preoccupation with imitation

[1] I leave out of consideration the De Dinarcho, for reasons explained above, pp. 37-8.

has led Dionysius to do less than justice in many respects to his author. Then again the rhetorical system supplies the framework of the essay, as it supplied the framework of the *De Demosthene*, though the proportion of mechanical criticism by ἀρεταί, which disfigures the critic's earliest work, is small. There are, however, two important respects in which Dionysius has progressed. In the first place, he is more thorough and more consistently detailed; he has grappled with the style of a difficult author and given illustration and analysis throughout; and his employment of the method of recasting is nearly twice as frequent as in the *De Demosthene*. In extent, therefore, rather than depth or penetration of analysis, he has advanced. Secondly, he has transferred to the sphere of subject-matter those virtues which he developed in the essays of the middle period which were devoted to style. Illustration and analysis, as well as the cultivation of a historical point of view, are here found in Dionysius' treatment of the πραγματικὸς τόπος, which is immeasurably superior in exposition to his earlier treatments of this subject. This latter development is of particular interest, for Dionysius intended to study the πραγματικὴ δεινότης of Demosthenes immediately after his essay on Thucydides, as well as the work of Aeschines and Hyperides, and if, as the opening words of the *De Dinarcho* rather suggest, these studies were actually composed, then it may well be that we have lost some of the maturest and most thorough of Dionysius' critical work.

CHAPTER VI

Conclusions

IT will have been observed from the foregoing chapters that throughout his critical works Dionysius was strongly influenced by the practical considerations of rhetorical imitation. The μίμησις principle is scarcely ever entirely abandoned; it had become firmly entrenched in Dionysius' mind in his earliest critical work, and in none of his major essays can it be said to have left no trace. The *De Imitatione*, which was probably Dionysius' earliest essay, was expressly designed as a handbook for the guidance of pupils in their selection of models, and the authors therein recommended for study are criticised purely for their rhetorical value (cf. pp. 39–40). Similarly the *De Lysia*, which followed, abounds in advice to the reader to imitate the many desirable qualities of Lysias' style, and is simply a fuller treatment of that author along the lines laid down in the previous work (cf. p. 43). The *De Isocrate* reveals similar characteristics; Isocrates' subject-matter and nobility of ideas are awarded high praise, whereas his style is considered to be unsuitable for imitation owing to its artificiality and lack of the power to stir (cf. pp. 48–9). The *De Isaeo*, being largely occupied with the comparison and contrast of Isaeus with Lysias and Demosthenes, is rather more free from this emphasis on μίμησις; but it is still part of the scheme for supplying advice on standard models (cf. p. 53). The *Epistula ad Ammaeum I*, too, being a study of a purely academic point, naturally lacks reference to the question of imitation; but in the first half of the *De Demosthene* (i.e. cc. 1–33) the critic's further stress on the shortcomings of Isocrates and his enthusiastic recommendation of Demosthenes as a model show that the rhetorical outlook was still predominant (cf. p. 61). It is only in the *De Compositione Verborum* and the latter half of the *De Demosthene* (i.e. cc. 34–58) that the principle of μίμησις tends to drop into the background; for although the former study is intended by its author as an aid to students of political oratory the investigation which it contains into the problem of style, and the subsequent application of the results thereof to Demosthenes, lead the critic into new paths where the delight of fresh discovery renders him for the time oblivious of practical issues. In the *Epistula ad Pompeium*, however, the inclusion of a fairly long excerpt from the *De Imitatione* suggests that Dionysius had by no means given up his interest in assessing the value of different models of prose style; and the *De Thucydide*, in which lists of speeches worthy of imitation are given, was clearly meant to serve a practical purpose and shows what misguided judgments can arise from the application of rhetorical principles to an author of a totally different genre (cf. pp. 81–2). Rhetoric, then, overhangs the critic like a cloud; sometimes it descends and darkens a whole essay; at other times it seems to lift, particularly when the critic is engaged upon some form of original research. But it cannot be said that there is any gradual improvement; for although in the *De Lysia* the precepts of imitation of virtues and avoidance of vices are more constantly reiterated than in the succeeding essays, yet in the *De Thucydide* the doctrine of imitation is still manifest throughout. Nor indeed can any permanent improvement be reasonably expected; so closely interwoven were rhetoric and criticism in the ancient world.

Similarly the ancient critic was compelled to set to work with the implements of rhetoric. From the beginning style had to be dissociated from subject-matter, vocabulary from composition, composition from figures; and the critic looked at his author through a number of prescribed lenses. Rarely did he see his author as a whole, and all too often his conclusions were but a collection of separately achieved results, lacking co-ordination and unity. Then again, the influence of traditional rules, handed down through generations of rhetoricians, and carrying ever more weight the longer they survived, could not fail to hamper the critic. If style must be this and that, no deviation from the rigid norm could win anything but censure. Dionysius was hampered from the first by the necessity of employing a system already complete and accepted without question among teachers of rhetoric. In nearly all his major essays, as a result, there is criticism according to the prescribed divisions and subdivisions. Criticism in the *De Imitatione* is particularly frigid and mechanical; we frequently perceive that Dionysius' remarks are based on such divisions as ἐκλογή as opposed to σύνθεσις, or ἦθος as opposed to πάθος, or on the system of virtues of style, which is fully set forth and applied in the criticism of Herodotus and Thucydides (cf. pp. 40–2). In the *De Lysia* not only does the system of virtues given in the *De Imitatione* form a quite obvious framework for cc. 2–10, but further subdivisions of separate ἀρεταί are introduced. Criticism of the πραγματικὸς τόπος also falls into the three divisions of εὕρεσις, κρίσις, and τάξις, and the rules of the rhetorical manuals are on occasion actually quoted as authority (cf. pp. 43–5). The sketch of Isocrates' style in the second and third chapters of the *De Isocrate* is likewise built up on the system of virtues, and further reliance on the rhetorical system is noticeable in the criticism of his style according to its ἐκλογή, its σύνθεσις, and its σχήματα (cf. pp. 49–50). In the *De Isaeo*, however, the treatment of questions of style is manifestly free from the hampering system, only one sentence being devoted to the stock ἀρεταί (see p. 53). In the first half of the *De Demosthene*, it is not the virtues (though these reappear in two places) but the types of style which supply the framework (cf. pp. 61–2); and the criticism of authors by types is taken a step farther by the appearance in the *De Compositione Verborum* and the latter half of the *De Demosthene* of the three types of composition; in the *De Comp. Verb.*, too, mechanical reliance on the system misleads the critic into supposing that any charm of style which is not due to ἐκλογή must be due to σύνθεσις (cf. p. 72). Finally, the *De Thucydide* reveals the influence of the system both in the discussion of subject-matter according to ὑπόθεσις, διαίρεσις, τάξις and ἐξεργασίαι, and in the setting forth of the subdivisions of the λεκτικὸς τόπος in c. 22 and the application thereof to criticism in the chapters immediately succeeding (cf. p. 84). In one respect, however, there is a gradual change; in the earlier essays, particularly the *De Imitatione* and the *De Lysia*, the system of stylistic virtues dominates the critic, whereas in the essays of the middle and later periods the critic has learnt to pay less attention to the stock virtues and to that extent at least dominates the system. It is noticeable, too, that when Dionysius feels an overmastering enthusiasm, as for Demosthenes (*De Dem.* c. 22), or a keen desire to capture and express in words some elusive quality, as the charm of Lysias (*De Lysia*, cc. 10–11), he forgets his rhetorical system and creates pure criticism on a far higher plane.

But despite these limitations of outlook and treatment there is noticeable in these essays a remarkable development in thoroughness of exposition. In the *De Imitatione* Dionysius is, as he informs us elsewhere, prevented by lack of space from illustrating his remarks; but those remarks, cast as they are into a very conventional mould, are quite superficial and reveal no indication whatsoever that the critic has made personal contact with the authors whom he criticises, or any really careful examination of their work. Such comparative criticism as there is in this essay is particularly frigid and mechanical, as may be seen, for instance, from the way in which the stylistic virtues and failings of Herodotus and Thucydides are listed (cf. pp. 41-2). A similar artificiality of treatment is noticeable in the *De Lysia*; here there is no reason why Dionysius should not have illustrated and explained his remarks instead of leaving them for un-disputed acceptance. The set παραδείγματα of Lysias' style are well chosen, but there is no attempt made as yet to substantiate individual points of criticism. Comparative criticism, too, is confined to occa-sional brief remarks, and there is no sign that the critic has begun to consider his author in the light of his possible relation to other writers of Greek prose. On the other hand, there is a welcome improvement in the tenth and eleventh chapters, in which for the first time the critic really attempts to get into touch with his author and to discover the secret of Lysias' unfailing charm (cf. pp. 47-8). In the *De Isocrate* a change begins to make itself felt; for Dionysius not only makes contact with his author in his appreciation of the nobility of Isocrates' ideas, but also feels the necessity of explaining his criticisms rather more fully. Accordingly, instead of being con-tent with choosing set passages for illustration, he also analyses in cc. 14 and 20 several sentences of Isocrates in order to reveal the artificiality which results from his excessive use of figures. His analysis does not, it is true, represent deep thought, but it shows that the critic has expended a little more effort than hitherto, and it renders his remarks more convincing and satisfying to the reader. His comparisons and contrasts, though occasionally well expressed, are not particularly well worked out, being still based on the system of virtues of style, as may be seen from c. 11 (cf. pp. 49 and 51-2). It is in the *De Isaeo* that comparative criticism comes to the fore as a valuable aid in explaining the characteristics of the author criticised, and in that essay the comparison and contrast of Isaeus with Lysias and Demosthenes is done quite without mechanical aid, and owes its success to the genuine effort made by the critic to bring out his points by illustration and analysis. Progress is also noticeable in the acknowledgment of the influence of Isaeus upon Demosthenes, which shows that Dionysius had now ceased to regard each author as a watertight compartment. In this essay, too, a valuable addition to the means of exposition is made when the process of recasting is for the first time introduced; for when Dionysius on two occasions rewrites sentences of Isaeus he leaves no doubt in the reader's mind about the points to which he objects. But it should be added that, despite these virtues of exposition, there are certain shortcomings; for, apart from the two passages where recasting is employed, Dionysius' comments tend to be of a somewhat general nature, and there is room for very considerable improvement in thoroughness and depth (cf. pp. 54–7). In the first half of the *De Demosthene* comparative criticism is paramount; Dionysius is by now so well acquainted with the styles of other orators, particularly Lysias and Isocrates, that he is able to compare and contrast them in a very interesting manner with Demosthenes, with a view to proving the latter's complete pre-eminence. Thucydides and Plato are also brought into the picture and the superiority of Demosthenes is likewise proclaimed. This investigation is naturally productive of extensive illustration and considerable analysis of individual passages; this analysis is deeper than in the *De Isocrate* and *De Isaeo*, and the exposition gains not a little by the further employment of the process of recasting, which appears on nine occasions (cf. pp. 62–70). The *De Compositione Verborum*, which was composed before the *De Demosthene* was complete, being a work of literary theory rather than criticism, does not stand on quite the same level as the preceding essays; but it plays an important part in the development of the critic's powers in that his researches into the nature and effects of good and bad composition lead him to examine his texts with still greater care; analysis is extended to individual words, syllables, and even letters, and recasting is employed to show how any disturbance of word-order ruins the effect of well-written passages. Dionysius' criticism is occasionally apt to suffer from his over-eagerness to prove the importance of σύνθεσις, but his study nevertheless helped further to develop his already considerable powers of analysis (cf. pp. 74–7). The value of his investigation is clearly seen in the latter half of the *De Demosthene*, where passages of Demosthenes are subjected to an even more detailed examination than in the first half of the essay (cf. pp. 77–8). The *Epistula ad Pompeium*, which was occasioned by the publication of the *De Demosthene*, is altogether too slight to reveal further development, but is interesting when viewed as a defence of the methods of comparison and contrast adopted in that essay (cf. pp. 78–9). Finally, the *De Thucydide*, together with its supplement, the *Epistula ad Ammaeum II*, represents the most thorough investigation into the style and subject-matter of any one author yet criticised. In this essay Dionysius has obviously applied himself far more closely and consistently to the actual text than in earlier studies, and as a result his work abounds in quotation and reference. One has only to compare the treatment of Thucydides' characteristics in *Epistula ad Ammaeum II* with the treatment of the style of Lysias, Isocrates, Isaeus, or Demosthenes in previous studies to realise how much more detailed an exposition is now given. Dionysius' analysis, too, is more frequent and more sustained, as may be well seen in his examination of Thuc. III, 82 in cc. 29 ff. (cf. pp. 88 ff.); and the method of recasting, always a good indication of the effort expended by the critic, is employed on some eighteen occasions. The historical approach is also seen at its best, the works of previous historians being considered before that of Thucydides himself, and comparative criticism appears both in this connection and in the closing chapters where the influence of Thucydides on Demosthenes is illustrated (cf. pp. 93–4). Lastly, the virtues of illustration and analysis hitherto only apparent in the study of style are here seen to advantage in the study of subject-matter, which in its detail far surpasses earlier efforts in this branch (cf. pp. 85–8). Taken as a whole, therefore, the critic's work on Thucydides represents the most thorough of his studies.

It is perhaps hardly necessary to say, in view of all this, that the real strength of Dionysius as a critic lies in his power of systematic study and analysis. He rarely gives expression to his personal feelings, though when he does so he is most impressive. There are, of course, dangers in the sole use of either method of criticism; analysis alone may never succeed in communicating to the reader those intangible qualities which refuse to surrender their secrets to examination; on the other hand, spontaneous expression of a critic's personal reactions may easily lead him into empty words that really convey very little.[1] It is worthy of notice that the ancient rhetorical schools considered it necessary for the critic to possess not only the rational but also the irrational instinct (ἄλογος αἴσθησις);[2] and they fully recognised that neither of the two was self-sufficient. An interesting recognition of the existence of these two diametrically opposed methods of criticism is given by Gibbon in his remarks on "Longinus".[3] "The ninth chapter", he says, "is one of the finest monuments of antiquity. Till now, I was acquainted only with two ways of criticising a beautiful passage: the one, to show, by an exact anatomy of it, the distinct beauties of it, and whence they sprung; the other, an idle exclamation, or a general encomium, which leaves nothing behind it. Longinus has shown me that there is a third. He tells me his own feelings upon reading it; and tells them with such energy, that he communicates them." Idle exclamations and general encomia might well be illustrated from much of Roman literary criticism. The expression of personal feeling is responsible for the lasting greatness of "Longinus". But for showing, by an exact anatomy, the distinct beauties, and whence they sprung, there is no critic of antiquity, whose work at any rate is extant, to compare with Dionysius of Halicarnassus.

[1] Cf. Saintsbury, *History of Criticism* (Edinburgh and London, 1890), I, p. 137 "not that she (viz. criticism) may not justly imp her wings for a higher flight now and then, but she must beware of flapping them in the inane".

[2] *De Thuc.* c. 27 (= I, 371) τό τε λογικὸν καὶ τὸ ἄλογον κριτήριον, ὑφ' ὧν ἀμφοτέρων ἀξιοῦμεν ἅπαντα κρίνεσθαι κατὰ τὰς τέχνας.

[3] *Journal*, Sept. 3, 1762 (cited by Roberts, *Longinus on the Sublime*[2] (Cambridge, 1907), p. 229).

BIBLIOGRAPHY

An almost complete bibliography of the *Scripta Rhetorica* up to and including the year 1900 is given by W. Rhys Roberts in his *Dionysius of Halicarnassus: the Three Literary Letters* (Cambridge, 1901), pp. 209–19. Of the editions there mentioned I have had those of Sylburg (1586), Reiske (1774–7), Gros (1826), and Usener-Radermacher (I, 1899 and II, 1904 and 1929) constantly by me. The editions of separate treatises by Upton (1702), Holwell (1766), Schaefer (1808), Goeller (1815), Krüger (1823), van Herwerden (1861), Roessler (1873), Usener (1889), and Desrousseaux-Egger (1890) have sometimes been of service. Of the occasional and periodical publications, I have used those of Busse (1841), Blass (1863 and 1865), Mestwerdt (1868), Wichmann (1878), Baudat (1879), Kaibel (1885), Liers (1886), Rohde (1886), Ammon (1889), Rabe (1893), Wilamowitz-Möllendorff (1899), Radermacher (1897 and 1899), Warren (1899), Heydenreich (1900), and Roberts (1897 and 1900). To Roberts' list should be added: (1) M. Mille, "Le Jugement de Denys d'Halicarnasse sur Thucydide" (*Annales de la Faculté des Lettres de Bordeaux*, 1889, pp. 83–101); (2) J. Denis, "Denys d'Halicarnasse, Jugement sur Lysias" (*Faculté des Lettres de Caen, Bulletin Mensuel*, 1890, pp. 165–70 and 176–89). The following list contains works on Dionysius published since 1901, apart from those of a purely textual nature:

EGGER, MAX. *Denys d'Halicarnasse, Essai sur la critique littéraire et la rhétorique chez les Grecs du siècle d'Auguste* (Paris, 1902).

RADERMACHER, L. Article "Dionysius" (Scripta Rhetorica) in Pauly-Wissowa's *Realencyclopädie*, V, 1 (1903).

VAN HOOK, LA RUE. *Metaphorical Terminology of Greek Rhetoric and Literary Criticism* (Chicago, 1905).

SMILEY, C. N. *Latinitas and Ἑλληνισμός* (University of Wisconsin, *Bulletin*, 1906), ch. II.

JOHNSTON, W. P. *Greek Literary Criticism* (Oxford, 1907), pp. 25–6.

KREMER, E. *Über das rhetorische System des Dionys von Halikarnass* (Strassburg, 1907).

KROLL, W. "Randbemerkungen" (*Rhein. Mus.* LXII (1907), pp. 82–101).

GEIGENMÜLLER, P. *Quaestiones Dionysianae de vocabulis artis criticae* (Leipzig, 1908).

TOLKIEHN, J. "Dionysios von Halikarnass und Caecilios von Calakte" (*W. kl. Ph.* 1908, pp. 84–6).

TUKEY, R. H. "A note on Dionysius" (*C.R.* XXIII (1909), pp. 187–9).

—— "The Composition of the *De Oratoribus Antiquis* of Dionysius" (*C.P.* IV (1909), pp. 390–404).

NASSAL, F. *Ästhetische-rhetorische Beziehungen zwischen Dionysius von Halicarnass und Cicero* (Tübingen, 1910).

ROBERTS, W. RHYS. *Dionysius of Halicarnassus, On Literary Composition* (London, 1910).

BREITENBACH, H. P. "The *De Comp. Verb.* of Dionysius of Halicarnassus considered with reference to the *Rhetoric* of Aristotle" (*C.P.* VI (1911), pp. 163–79).

STROUX, J. *De Theophrasti virtutibus dicendi* (Leipzig, 1912), pp. 72–80 and 108 ff.

GALLI, U. "L' opera rhetorica di Dionigi d' Alicarnasso" (*St. It. F.* XIX (1912), pp. 237 ff.).

HUBBELL, H. M. *The Influence of Isocrates on Cicero, Dionysius and Aristides* (Yale and O.U.P. 1914), pp. 41–53.

MEERWALDT, J. D. *De Dionysiana virtutum et generum dicendi doctrina* (= *Studia ad generum dicendi historiam pertinentia*, 1), Amsterdam, 1920.

DENNISTON, J. D. *Greek Literary Criticism* (London, 1924), ch. V.

KALINKA, E. "Die Arbeitsweise des Rhetors Dionys, I" (*Wien. Stud.* XLIII (1924), pp. 157–68).

—— "Die Arbeitsweise des Rhetors Dionys, II" (*Wien. Stud.* XLIV (1925), pp. 46–68).

ROBERTS, W. RHYS. *Greek Rhetoric and Literary Criticism* (London and N.Y. 1928), ch. IV.

LOCKWOOD, J. F. "ΗΘΙΚΗ ΛΕΞΙΣ and Dinarchus" (*C.Q.* XXIII (1929) pp. 180–5).

ATKINS, J. W. H. *Literary Criticism in Antiquity* (Cambridge, 1934), vol. II, ch. III.

PAVANO, G. "Dionisio d' Alicarnasso, critico di Tucidide" (*Memorie della Reale Accademia delle Scienze di Torino*, LXVII, 1935–6).

LOCKWOOD, J. F. "The Metaphorical Terminology of Dionysius of Halicarnassus" (*C.Q.* XXXI (1937), pp. 192 ff.).

BONNER, S. F. "Dionysius of Halicarnassus and the Peripatetic Mean of Style" (*C.P.* XXXIII (1938), pp. 257–66).

INDEX

Printed in the United States
By Bookmasters